AF582362

Throttle & Lipstick

RAANI RAFTAAR

To all those who balance life on two wheels!

"The road doesn't judge who you are or where you've come from; it only asks that you show up and ride. Every mile teaches you something, every journey shapes you, and every turn is a step closer to the person you're becoming."

Acknowledgments

This journey, both on and off the road, would not have been possible without the incredible support of so many people and places that shaped me along the way.

To my parents, thank you for being my anchor, even as I took roads less travelled. Your belief in me has been my driving force through every twist and turn.

To my friends, my first road companions, and my closest confidants—thank you. My college friends, who introduced me to the thrill of biking, were there to teach me the ropes and push me beyond my limits.

To all my biker friends and the inspiring women in the community, you've shown me camaraderie, resilience, and passion that go beyond words. You are the heart of this journey.

A special acknowledgment to my bikes: my loyal Honda Unicorn, which first taught me the freedom of the road; my second-hand Karizma, which brought unexpected adventures; and my beloved Iron 883, which has been with me through so much, roaring through challenges and giving me direction. Each of you—machines in form but companions in spirit—played a role in helping me discover my strength and resilience.

To the roads that tested me, the ones that scared me, and the ones that comforted me, thank you for giving me purpose. To the destinations that brought peace, growth, and moments of clarity, and the places I rested, thank you for welcoming me. The people I met along the way—whether strangers who became friends or brief encounters that left a lasting impact—each of you has enriched this journey beyond measure.

Finally to you, the reader, thank you for picking up this book, for allowing me to share this journey with you. I hope you find pieces of your own story here, and that it inspires you to explore, to dream, and to discover your own path. The road awaits, and it's a privilege to travel it with kindred spirits like you.

With all my gratitude,
Raani Raftaar

The Open Road Beckons

There's something almost sacred about the quiet before dawn. The world sits still, suspended in that delicate balance between night and day, waiting for the sun to break the horizon and breathe life into it again. It was in this suspended moment that I found myself—standing beside my Harley Davidson Iron 883, feeling the cool, damp air cling to my skin. The bike, hulking and silent beside me, felt like an extension of my body, as much a part of me as my own heart. Its weight was comforting, solid, and constant in a way few things had ever been.

The key slipped into the ignition, and with a firm push of the start switch, the machine rumbled to life. The sound wasn't just a mechanical growl; it was the pulse of freedom reverberating through my chest, matching the steady thud of my heartbeat. It was the sound of infinite possibilities, of open roads and uncharted horizons. And for me, it was the sound of belonging. Out here, on the back of my Harley, I was truly home.

The morning air was crisp, biting in the way early autumn mornings often are. It nipped at the exposed skin of my neck as I zipped up my jacket and settled into the seat. The liner beneath the jacket was warm, having been softened by countless rides, and as I tightened my grip on the handlebars, a familiar sense of anticipation buzzed through my veins.

In front of me, the road stretched on for miles, an endless ribbon of asphalt cutting through the still, misty landscape. The sky above was painted in soft pinks and golds, the sun peeking over the edge of the earth as if unsure whether to rise or not. The trees lining the road stood like silent witnesses, their leaves beginning to turn the burnt orange and fiery red of the coming season. I took a deep breath, filling my lungs with the earthy scent of wet leaves and freshly turned soil, and for the first time that day, I smiled.

Out here, I was free. There was no weight of judgment, no eyes scrutinizing me, no questions of who I was or who I was supposed to be. The road didn't care about gender or identity. It didn't ask questions or pass judgment. It simply stretched out in front of me, offering endless possibilities with every turn, every mile.

The low hum of the Harley beneath me was soothing, like a lullaby for the restless parts of my soul. As I slowly rolled onto the road and twisted the throttle, the machine came alive in my hands. The roar of the engine filled the quiet morning air, a sound so familiar and comforting that it felt like coming home. The vibrations coursed through me, grounding me in the moment, reminding me that out here, I wasn't running from anything. I was simply existing—free, unburdened, and whole.

But it hadn't always been like this. The open road had called to me long before I transitioned, back when I was still navigating the confusion and weight of an identity I hadn't yet embraced. Back then, riding had been an escape. I would climb onto my bike—then a Honda Unicorn—and ride until the world blurred around me, until the noise in my head silenced, and the tightness in my chest loosened just enough for me to breathe. In those days, I didn't fully understand who I was or what I was searching for. I only knew that out on the road, with the wind whipping past me and the roar of the engine in my ears, I could forget for a while. I could disappear into the speed and the thrill of the ride, leaving behind the confusion and the pain that constantly followed me.

But that was years ago. The person I was back then—the young man who never felt quite comfortable in his own skin—felt distant now, like a shadow of a life that no longer fit.

That version of me had been a half-formed idea, a puzzle with pieces that didn't quite fit together. Riding back then had been my escape from a reality that felt wrong, but now, it was my liberation.

As I shifted gears, feeling the familiar surge of power beneath me, a smile tugged at the corners of my lips. No matter how many times I did this, the thrill of it never faded. My Harley was more than just a machine—it was an extension of me, the embodiment of strength and resilience. I had named it *Falcon*, after the mighty bird of prey that always fascinated me with its grace, strength, and freedom. In many ways, this bike had been with me through every twist and turn of my life, from my college years as a confused young boy to the woman I had fought to become. It had witnessed my dilemma, carried my burdens and more than once, it had saved me.

The road ahead stretched on endlessly, disappearing into the horizon, and with it came memories. Flashes of a different time, when life had felt simpler but infinitely heavier. I remembered those early college days, the ones where I had first fallen in love with motorcycles. Back then, it had been the freedom, the control, and the sheer power of the bikes that drew me in. I would watch, mesmerized, as a group of fellow students spent their weekends customizing their motorcycles and racing them just outside of the city of Bengaluru. I wasn't part of their group, not at first, but I admired them from a distance. There was something about the way they moved, the way they commanded the bikes with such ease, that made me want to be like them.

It wasn't long before I convinced my parents to buy me a bike of my own—a Honda Unicorn. It wasn't the flashiest or the fastest bike, but it was mine. And when I rode it, I felt alive in a way that nothing else in my life could make me feel. But those days of confusion and disconnection seemed far away now, like a distant echo I could barely hear. I had come a long way since then. I had fought for the person I was now, the woman who sat on the saddle of this Harley, proud and unapologetically herself.

I pulled to the side of the road and cut the engine, letting the sudden silence wrap around me. It was a stillness that was almost jarring, wrapping around me like a thick blanket. I could hear the soft rustle of leaves in the trees, the distant chirp of birds waking with the sun. I leaned back, pulling off my helmet and the balaclava, letting the cool air touch my face.

The sun had risen higher now, casting a warm glow over everything. It was one of those mornings where the air felt charged with possibility, where the day ahead seemed to stretch out with endless promises. There was something about the solitude of the open road that allowed me to reflect in ways that daily life didn't always allow. Out here, with nothing but the hum of the engine and the vast sky above me, I could connect with myself on a deeper level. I could let go of the distractions, the noise, and the chaos of the world and simply be.

As I gazed over the horizon, memories flooded back to that first ride after I had transitioned. The experience had been both familiar and profoundly new. My body, transformed by the journey I had chosen, felt different in ways that were unmistakable yet deeply a part of me. My hips had softened and curved, lending a new balance to my stance; my arms, now slender and refined, held the handlebars with a graceful strength. And my chest, with its newfound weight, subtly reminded me of the changes that had shaped me, inside and out.

There was a fleeting moment of doubt—would I still connect with the bike, feel that visceral thrill? But as soon as the engine came to life, those worries dissolved. I found not only the same exhilaration but an even deeper sense of unity between my body and the bike, as if we were rediscovering the road together.But the moment I sat down, all those doubts melted away. The bike responded to me just as it always had, its powerful hum vibrating through me as if nothing had changed. Riding wasn't about escape anymore. It wasn't about running away from who I was or what I felt. Now, it was about embracing who I had become. It was about claiming my space in the world, owning the person that I had always been beneath the skin.

I ran my fingers along the smooth metal of the Harley's gas tank, feeling the coolness of the surface beneath my fingertips. Riding a bike had helped me so much—through every hard-won battle, every tear shed, and every moment of doubt. It had been my constant go to when I had nothing else, and in many ways, it had helped me find my way back to myself.

The road in front of me beckoned. It whispered promises of adventure, of freedom, of the unknown. But for now, I was content to sit and breathe in the present. I had fought so hard to become the person I was, and for the first time in my life, I wasn't running from myself or my past. The woman I had become was strong, proud, and free—both on and off my Harley. And the journey ahead, well, that was just beginning.

An Unexpected Love

The first time I stepped off the bus in Bengaluru, the air felt alive. It was electric, buzzing with the sounds of a city that never seemed to sleep. The roar of engines was everywhere—on every street corner, at every traffic light, and weaving through the bustling roads like a river of steel and speed. The sweet hums of Hondas, the creaky sound of the yesteryear Yamahas, the thumps of the Royal Enfields and the mellowed roars of the TVS and Bajaj, Bengaluru had it all. It was home to the Jawas, RD350s and many other bikes that had withered away with time, but still cemented a strong place in the hearts of the enthusiasts. The city wasn't just a backdrop; it was a living, breathing entity with its own pulse, and motorcycles were its heartbeat. The sights, sounds, and smells of the city hit me all at once—the blend of exhaust fumes, spices from street food vendors, and the faint, almost forgotten scent of rain on hot asphalt.

I'd come to Bengaluru to study engineering, but as soon as I arrived, it became clear that this city had other plans for me. My dreams had been small when I arrived, my focus purely on passing exams and getting a degree. But Bengaluru had a way of turning even the most straightforward paths into unexpected journeys. It wasn't long before I found myself being drawn into a world I'd only ever admired from a distance—the world of motorcycles.

I had always watched motorcycles from afar, admiring their sleek lines and the way they seemed to glide through traffic with effortless grace. But here, in Bengaluru, motorcycles weren't just admired—they were revered. It didn't take long for me to notice the culture surrounding them. In this city, motorcycles were more than just vehicles. They were a lifestyle, a passion, and for some, an obsession. The riders here moved with a confidence and freedom I had never known, and I couldn't help but want to be a part of it.

The first time I saw the garage, I had no idea it would become a second home to me. Tucked away in a corner of the campus, it looked unassuming—a simple, nondescript shed where a few students gathered on weekends to work on their bikes. I had seen them from a distance at first, a small group of seniors who spent hours under the hood, their hands blackened with grease, their faces focused with a kind of intensity that was both intimidating and alluring. The origins of this shed dates back to the late 90s when my college had just started its curriculum. A group of mechanical engineering students had converted this shed into a garage, which was originally meant to be a shed for the workers involved in the construction of the college. The utility of this garage was to be a space for the final year projects of mechanical engineering students and this tradition continued!

The garage also accommodated anyone and everyone who wanted to play with engines or anything mechanical. So, it welcomed bikers! They weren't just casual riders. They were the kind of people who lived and breathed motorcycles. They spoke in a language I didn't yet understand—discussing carburetors, sprockets, gear ratios, and custom exhaust systems as if they were talking about old friends. Their bikes weren't just modes of transportation; they were projects, works of art in progress, constantly being tweaked and improved for performance and speed. I watched them from afar, mesmerized, and before long, I found myself drawn to their world.

One Saturday afternoon, I finally worked up the courage to approach them. I still remember how the air smelled of gasoline and hot rubber as I stepped into the garage, the clang of tools and the low hum of engines providing a kind of rhythm to their work. Konark, one of the seniors, also my neighbour in the hostel, looked up from the bike he was working on and smiled when he saw me standing there, awkward and unsure. We shared a lot of things in common starting from the family background, schooling and interests which we got to know at a later stage in college.

"You want to help?" he asked, tossing me a wrench.

And just like that, I was in.

For the next few weeks, I became a regular in the garage. I wasn't much help at first, mostly standing to the side and handing tools to the more experienced guys, but I was learning. They taught me the basics—how engines worked, how to change the oil, how to swap out brake pads. Each weekend, I left the garage feeling more confident, more connected to something bigger than myself. The smell of grease and gasoline had become comforting, and the sight of a perfectly tuned engine was nothing short of beautiful.

But it wasn't just the technical aspects of motorcycles that drew me in—it was the camaraderie. The guys in the garage became more than just fellow students. They became friends, brothers in a sense, bound together by mutual love for bikes and the thrill of the open road. They didn't care about my past, my struggles, or the confusion that constantly clouded my thoughts. All that mattered was that I was there, learning, growing, and becoming part of their world.

One Saturday, everything changed.

We were in the middle of a typical garage session when Konark tossed me a set of keys. "Take her for a spin," he said, nodding towards an old LML Adreno that was parked near the door.

The bike was silver, its paint chipped and faded, with yellow stickers on the fender that had long since lost their shine. It wasn't the prettiest bike in the garage, but to me, it was perfect. I froze. Up until that moment, I had never actually ridden a motorcycle. I had watched them for years, studied their every movement, and learned how they worked, but I had never been the one behind the handlebars. The thought of riding both excited and terrified me.

"Come on, you'll be fine," Konark urged. "Just take it slow."

My heart pounded in my chest as I took the keys from his outstretched hand. I climbed onto the bike, feeling the weight of it beneath me, and gripped the handlebars. The metal was cool under my fingers, and the leather seat was worn but comfortable. The engine was silent for now, but I could feel its potential, like a sleeping giant waiting to be awakened.

With a deep breath, I kicked the engine to life. The bike sputtered for a moment before roaring awake, the vibrations running through my body like a shot of adrenaline. I felt alive.

My hands trembled slightly as I twisted the throttle and eased off the clutch. The bike lurched forward, and for a moment, I thought I might lose control. But then, as I found the rhythm between the clutch and throttle, the bike began to move smoothly down the road. The wind whipped past me, cool and refreshing against my skin, and the sound of the engine was a steady hum in my ears.

It felt like flying.

The world around me seemed to blur as I picked up speed, the city fading into the background as the road stretched out before me. Every twist of the throttle sent a surge of power through the bike, and I felt an indescribable sense of freedom. For the first time in my life, I wasn't running from something—I was moving towards something. Towards a future where I could be who I truly was, without fear or hesitation.

By the time I returned to the garage, my heart was racing, and my face was flushed with excitement. The guys clapped me on the back, congratulating me on my first ride, but I barely heard them. All I could think about was the feeling of the bike beneath me, the wind in my face, and the freedom that came with it.

I was hooked.

From that day on, motorcycles became more than just a hobby—they became a passion, an obsession even. I spent every spare moment in the garage, learning everything I could about bikes, pushing myself to ride faster, harder, and with more precision. The guys in the garage became my mentors, teaching me the finer details of riding and customization. I learned how to fine-tune the suspension, how to adjust the carburetor for optimal performance, and how to balance the power of the engine with the handling of the bike.

But as I spent more time on the bike, something else began to shift inside me. Riding wasn't just about the speed or the thrill of the open road—it was about the freedom it gave me. Freedom from the expectations of others, from the confusion that had plagued me for so long. When I was on the bike, I wasn't thinking about my body or my identity—I was just *me*. Free, powerful, and completely in control.

The more I rode, the more I realized that motorcycles weren't just machines—they were metaphors for the journey I was on. Each ride was a new challenge, a new opportunity to push myself and see how far I could go. And as I mastered the bike, I began to master myself.

I knew then that my love for motorcycles wasn't just a passing phase—it was part of who I was, part of the person I was becoming. And as I sped down the open road, the wind whipping through my hair and the sound of the engine roaring in my ears, I felt a sense of peace that I had never known before.

The road ahead was long, winding, and full of unknowns. But for the first time in my life, I wasn't afraid of what lay ahead. Because I knew that no matter what challenges came my way, I would face them with the same strength and determination that I had found on the back of that old LML Adreno.

The road was mine. And I was ready for whatever came next.

Strength From Riding

Riding a motorcycle, for me, has always been about more than just transportation. It was my sanctuary, my escape, my place of power. Each time I twisted the throttle and felt the engine rumble beneath me, I became something more than just a person on a machine. I became weightless, unbound by the expectations that the world had placed on me. The road stretched ahead, a blank canvas, and as the miles blurred into one another, I felt free. Free from judgment, free from the labels that society had tried to put on me, free from the constraints of identity that had always felt too small, too confining.

There is a unique power that comes with riding a motorcycle. It's not just the speed or the thrill of danger, although those play their part. It's the feeling of control, the knowledge that at that moment, you are the master of something strong, powerful, and untamed. You feel the engine roar to life, the hum of the machine vibrating through your body, a reminder that you and the bike are one entity. Every movement, every subtle shift in weight or pressure on the handlebars, alters the course of the journey.

I remember the first time I felt that rush of power, that absolute sense of control. The first time I revved the engine of a bike—really *revved* it—felt like setting loose something wild inside me, a force that had been hidden, repressed, waiting for the right moment to be unleashed. There was something primal in it, something raw, a feeling that I had been craving for years without realizing it. In a world where I had always felt out of place, unsure of myself and my identity, riding a motorcycle gave me something concrete to hold onto. On the bike, there were no questions about who I was or wasn't. It was just me, the road, and the hum of the machine beneath me.

Riding a bike gave me strength—not just physical strength, though the demands of controlling such a powerful machine are undeniable. It gave me an inner strength, a sense of self-assuredness that I had never felt before. Each time I mounted the bike, I felt like I was stepping into a different version of myself, a version that was more confident, more capable, more *me*. The world outside seemed to fade when I was on my bike. The noise, the pressure, the expectations—they all disappeared, drowned out by the roar of the engine and the wind rushing past me. It was in these moments that I felt invincible, untouchable, as if I were riding through time itself, breaking free of the constraints of the present and the future. The bike wasn't just a machine; it was a conduit for freedom, for possibility.

Of course, there was danger too. Every time I climbed onto the seat of a motorcycle, there was a part of me that knew I was stepping into something risky, something that could end in disaster with just one wrong move. And that danger thrilled me.
It's strange, isn't it? How the very thing that can kill you is also the thing that makes you feel most alive. Maybe that's part of the allure of motorcycles—the awareness of mortality, of how fragile life is, comes into sharp focus when you're riding at high speeds, the world flashing by in a blur. One slip, one miscalculation, and everything could be over. But that's what makes it *real*. The stakes are higher, and with that, the rewards feel more profound.

There were times, especially during the early days of my riding, when I wondered if clinging to something so traditionally "manly" as motorcycle riding was my way of trying to fight off my gender dysphoria. Maybe, I thought, if I embraced something dangerous, something powerful, something that society viewed as inherently masculine, it would help me resolve the conflict within myself. Maybe it would make me feel more at home in my skin.

But riding didn't solve my dysphoria. Instead, it did something better—it gave me a place where the questions didn't matter. On the bike, I didn't have to think about my identity or how I fit into the world. I didn't have to analyze every thought or feeling or wonder how it aligned with society's expectations. When I was riding, none of that mattered. The only thing that mattered was the road ahead and the freedom that came with it.

There's something almost meditative about riding alone on an open road. The hum of the engine becomes a constant backdrop, a rhythmic drone that lulls your mind into a kind of stillness. It was during these solo rides that I found the most clarity. While others might turn to quiet moments of reflection or meditation to find answers to life's questions, I found mine on the back of a motorcycle, hurtling down highways with nothing but the wind and the horizon to keep me company.

When I rode alone, everything became clear. I wasn't distracted by the noise of the world or the expectations of others. Instead, the world around me blurred, and my thoughts began to flow freely. Problems that had seemed insurmountable in the chaos of everyday life suddenly had solutions, as if the very act of riding was untangling the knots in my mind. The road was my therapist, and the bike was the tool that helped me access the deeper parts of my subconscious.

I remember one particular ride during my first year of college. I had been struggling with a decision—something personal, something that felt impossible to resolve. The weight of it sat heavy on my chest, clouding my thoughts, making everything else feel distant and unimportant. That night, unable to sleep, I borrowed a bike from one of my seniors and rode out into the night. It was a spontaneous decision, one that felt almost reckless at the time, but as soon as I hit the road, I knew it was the right one.

The streets were nearly empty, the city asleep around me as I rode through its veins. The sky above was dark, dotted with stars that seemed impossibly far away, and the air was cool against my skin. As I rode, the tension in my chest began to ease. The farther I went, the lighter I felt, as if the weight of the world was slowly lifting off my shoulders with every mile I put behind me.

By the time I returned home a few hours later, the solution to my problem had become clear. The answer had been there all along, buried beneath the noise and the confusion, and it had only taken the solitude of the road to bring it to the surface.

While solo rides gave me clarity and peace, the rides I shared with my friends were equally memorable, though for different reasons. There's something magical about riding with a group—knowing that you're part of something larger than yourself, that you're sharing an experience with people who understand the joy and freedom that comes with riding.

During my first year of college, my friends and I would often borrow bikes and go on impromptu rides to nearby places. None of us owned bikes, but we managed to scrounge up enough rides between us to make it work. We rode to Nandi Hills before sunrise, the road winding through lush greenery, the mist still hanging in the air as we climbed higher and higher, just to witness the sunset and savour a plate of Maggi noodles. We stopped at cafes on Mysore Road for late-night coffee runs, the cold air biting at our skin as we sipped steaming cups of tea and laughed about the adventures of the day. Although, these coffee rides weren't frequent as we didn't have enough money to buy coffee, since we poofed up everything in the fuel expenses.

Some of the best memories I have are from those rides—spur-of-the-moment decisions to hit the road, no destination in mind, just the desire to ride. One night, we decided to ride out for paranthas at a roadside dhaba. It was well past midnight, the roads nearly deserted, and the only sound was the rumble of our bikes as we sped through the darkness. The ride wasn't about where we were going or what we were doing. It was about the journey, about the shared experience of freedom and adventure.

Riding a bike didn't just give me freedom—it taught me things about myself that I might never have discovered otherwise. It taught me resilience, the ability to keep going even when things were tough. There were times when I felt like giving up, like the weight of the world was too much to bear. But every time I got on my bike, I was reminded of my strength, of my ability to push through whatever challenges life threw my way.

Riding also taught me the importance of balance—both literally and metaphorically. On a bike, balance is everything. One wrong move, one moment of hesitation, and everything can go wrong. But when you find that perfect balance, when you trust yourself and the machine beneath you, there's a kind of harmony that can't be found anywhere else.

That sense of balance, of trusting myself and my instincts, carried over into other aspects of my life. It helped me navigate the challenges of college, of relationships, of understanding my own identity. Most importantly, riding taught me that strength doesn't always come from conforming to expectations. It doesn't come from fitting into the boxes that society tries to put us in. True strength comes from knowing who you are, from embracing the parts of yourself that make you different, and from finding freedom in those differences.

Even now, years after those first rides in college, the love I have for motorcycles has never waned. It has become a part of who I am, woven into the fabric of my identity.

My college years in Bengaluru were a time of conflicting identities, of two separate worlds colliding—worlds that I wasn't sure could coexist. On one hand, there was the Naina Menon who had been assigned male at birth and on the other, the engineering student whose interest in motorcycles was beginning to border on obsession. The rumble of engines, the rush of speed, and the camaraderie of weekend garage sessions with fellow riders filled me with a sense of freedom I had never experienced before. Somewhere inside me, there was the real me—the Naina who existed quietly and secretly in the shadows, hidden from the world but bursting to come alive.

This chapter of my life, between 2005 and 2010, was one of clandestine explorations, as I walked a fine line between discovering my identity and protecting the façade that I was forced to maintain. I was a boy in a boy's hostel, surrounded by friends who would have never understood the depth of my inner conflict.

By day, I was just another student, attending lectures and working on projects. But whenever I had time, I was someone else entirely—a girl learning how to be herself, piece by piece, through trial and error. A girl who, through the anonymity of social media and the isolation of her room, was building the courage to embrace the woman she always knew she was.

It started innocently enough—being curious about the frock in my mum's almirah and a strange attraction to her velvet blouse and saree. In college, I had the freedom of buying whatever I wanted with the pocket money that I saved. Saving wasn't easy, everything was hand to mouth. Still, I managed to save some money to buy a velvet salwar kameez which was available at a discount since it was out of fashion and the cheapest saree that I could buy. The weight of these outfits were immense. It was a secret I would have to carry, something I would need to hide with meticulous care from the eyes of my hostel roommates.

That saree was the beginning of something larger. Over time, I began to collect more outfits—a salwar kameez here, a saree blouse there—each item tucked carefully into a hidden corner of my wardrobe or inside an old suitcase I rarely opened. The hostel, with its cramped rooms and lack of privacy, wasn't exactly the ideal place to explore one's femininity. But I found ways to indulge in secret moments of freedom. Late at night, when everyone else had fallen asleep, I would quietly slip out of my usual clothes and drape myself in the soft fabric of a saree or slip into a simple dress. In those moments, I could breathe.

The first time I wore a blouse fit to my size, I felt an odd mix of excitement and guilt. The snug fit across my chest, the gentle curve of the neckline—it felt right, like the missing piece of a puzzle falling into place. But it also felt like a betrayal. I was supposed to be a boy, after all, and boys didn't wear blouses. Boys didn't buy sarees or try on lingerie in the dead of the night. Or at least, that's what I had always been told.

But in the quiet solitude of my room, I didn't feel like a boy at all. I felt like Naina—soft, feminine, and alive. The clothes gave me a sense of belonging, a tangible connection to the person I knew I was inside. They were more than just clothes. They were ways for me to reclaim my identity, even if I could only do it in the privacy of my room.

During those years, social media was becoming a lifeline for people like me—people who lived double lives, who couldn't express their true selves in the real world but found solace in the anonymity of the internet. It was through platforms like Orkut and Facebook that I began to explore my femininity more openly, albeit in virtual spaces.
In the early days of Orkut, I created a profile under a pseudonym—a name that felt closer to who I really was than the one I had been given at birth. I joined groups for crossdressers and trans people, spaces where people shared stories, offered advice, and provided support.

It was in these online communities that I learned I wasn't alone. There were others like me, people struggling with the same feelings of dysphoria, the same desires to wear feminine clothes, the same fear of being discovered.
Through Orkut and later Facebook, I began connecting with like-minded people, some of whom were also exploring their gender identities. We exchanged messages late into the night when the network providers gave us 100 SMS per day, discussing everything from makeup tips to blouse sizes, from the best places to buy lingerie discreetly to how to hide feminine clothes in a hostel filled with boys. These conversations were my lifeline. They were the only place where I could be fully honest about who I was and what I was feeling.

In the real world, I was careful to keep my secrets well hidden. I continued to present myself as male, as was expected of me, attending classes, riding motorcycles with friends, and maintaining the façade of a “normal” boy. But online, I allowed myself to be Naina. I shared grainy pictures of me in the clothes I had bought, asked for advice on how to style a sari, and even experimented with makeup tutorials that I would never dare try in my hostel room.

It was through these virtual friendships that I learned the nuances of femininity. I discovered what blouse sleeves and style looked best on me, which fabric felt most comfortable against my skin, and how to style a dupatta in a way that felt elegant and natural. These small, seemingly insignificant details became incredibly important to me. They were pieces of the puzzle that made me feel whole, even if only for a brief moment.

While I was quietly discovering my feminine side behind closed doors, there was another passion growing in my life—one that couldn’t have been more different from the soft fabrics and delicate makeup I was exploring in private. That passion was motorcycles.

Riding a motorcycle gave me something I hadn't known I was missing—a sense of control, of power, of being fully present in the moment. The roar of the engine beneath me, the wind rushing past my face, the feel of the handlebars in my hands—it was intoxicating. Riding a bike wasn't just about transportation for me. It was a way to escape, a way to outrun the confusion and dysphoria that constantly lingered in the background of my mind.

My friends and I didn't own our own bikes during our first year of college, but that didn't stop us. We borrowed bikes from seniors, pooling our resources to go on impromptu rides to places like Nandi Hills or late-night cafes on Mysore Road. These rides became our way of escaping the pressures of academic life. But for me, they were also a way of escaping something deeper—my internal struggle with gender identity.

On those rides, as we raced down highways and navigated winding roads, I felt invincible. The speed, the danger, the thrill of it all—it was the perfect distraction. On a bike, I didn't have to think about who I was or what I was hiding. I was just another rider, part of the group, free from the constant mental battle of trying to fit into a world that didn't understand me.

But the more I rode, the more I began to realize that my passion for motorcycles wasn't entirely separate from my journey of self-discovery. In fact, the two were deeply connected. Riding a bike gave me the same sense of freedom that I felt when I wore feminine clothes in private. Both passions, though seemingly contradictory, offered me an escape from the constraints of societal expectations. In one world, I was learning how to be Naina—how to dress, how to carry myself, how to embrace my femininity. In the other world, I was learning how to ride a bike—how to navigate bad roads, how to balance speed and control, how to maintain the machine that gave me the freedom I craved. As I moved through my college years, I began to realize that these two passions—riding motorcycles and exploring my feminine identity—weren't as different as they seemed. They were, in fact, two sides of the same coin. Both offered me a sense of freedom, a way to escape the confines of the person I was expected to be.

When I was riding, I felt powerful, in control. The roar of the engine beneath me, the rush of wind against my skin—it was a reminder that I could command something as powerful and dangerous as a motorcycle. And yet, in those private moments when I slipped into a saree or tried on a new blouse, I felt a different kind of power.

It wasn't the power of speed or control—it was the power of being myself, of embracing the softness and femininity that I had always felt inside. Both passions were rooted in curiosity and excitement. On one hand, I was constantly experimenting with clothes—learning what styles suited me, figuring out my blouse size, discovering which fabrics made me feel most comfortable. On the other hand, I was learning the nuances of motorcycle maintenance—how to change the oil, how to adjust the brakes, how to handle a bike on bad roads. Each new discovery, whether in fashion or in mechanics, felt like a small victory, a step closer to understanding who I really was.

In a way, my journey through college was like riding a motorcycle. There were moments of speed and thrill, moments where everything seemed to fall into place and I felt like I was racing towards something greater. But there were also moments of danger, moments where I had to slow down.

In a way, my journey through college was like riding a motorcycle. There were moments of speed and thrill, moments where everything seemed to fall into place and I felt like I was racing towards something greater. But there were also moments of danger, moments where I had to slow down, recalibrate, and navigate difficult terrain.

Both riding and discovering my femininity brought challenges that I hadn't anticipated. Hiding my clothing in the hostel was no small feat, and I lived in constant fear of being discovered.

Every time I snuck out to buy a new piece of clothing, I was hyper-aware of the people around me, afraid that someone might recognize me or ask too many questions. Even in the privacy of my room, I was always on edge, listening for footsteps outside my door, ready to throw off the saree and stuff it back into its hiding place at a moment's notice.

But the same tension that came with hiding my femininity was present in riding a bike as well. There were dangers on the road, risks I had to take each time I rode, especially during those late-night trips with my friends when the roads were dark and empty, and the only thing keeping me steady was my grip on the handlebars. The thrill of speed, the rush of adrenaline—it was addictive, but it also reminded me of how fragile life was. One wrong turn, one patch of gravel, and it could all come crashing down.

It was the same with my identity. One wrong move, one person discovering my secret, and everything I had worked so hard to hide could unravel. And yet, despite the danger, I kept riding. I kept exploring my femininity. Because both gave me a sense of purpose, a sense of connection to myself that I couldn't find anywhere else.

Riding a bike gave me strength, but so did embracing my femininity. The two passions weren't separate—they were intertwined, each feeding into the other, each helping me grow into the person I was meant to be.

As I continued through my college years, I became adept at balancing these two worlds. By day, I was a student and a rider, surrounded by friends who only knew one side of me. By night, I was Naina, exploring my femininity in secret, connecting with others like me through the anonymity of the internet.

It was a dual life, and though it wasn't always easy, I found comfort in it. Riding gave me the strength to keep going, to face the challenges of hiding my true self in a world that didn't yet understand. And my feminine identity gave me the hope that one day, I would be able to live as my true self—fully, unapologetically, and without fear.
But for now, I had to keep both worlds separate. I couldn't let my friends know about the hidden clothes in my wardrobe or the late-night conversations I had with other trans women on Orkut and Facebook. I couldn't let them see the struggle beneath the surface, the constant push and pull between the person I was and the person I was becoming.

In the end, both riding and exploring my femininity became my salvation. They gave me something to hold onto when the world felt too heavy, when the weight of hiding my identity threatened to overwhelm me. Riding a bike was more than just a passion—it was a metaphor for my journey, a reminder that no matter how difficult the road ahead, I could keep going. And one day, I knew, I would no longer have to hide.

One day, Naina would be free.

Unicorn

The sun hung low in the sky, casting a golden glow over the coconut trees and quiet streets of Kerala. The warm light bathed everything in a peaceful stillness, but inside me, there was no stillness—only fire. A burning desire for something I had longed for, something that now gleamed in the distance: a 150cc Honda Unicorn.

The Honda Unicorn wasn't just a motorcycle. It was freedom. Sleek, black with elegant grey stripes, its gleaming body felt like the culmination of a long-fought battle. At 18, standing on the threshold of adulthood, it represented independence, adventure, and control over my own life. But like all dreams, it came with a price: the battle to convince my parents.

In an Indian family, nothing is simple, especially when it involves something as dangerous as a motorcycle. To my parents, bikes were the definition of risk. My father, a pragmatic man, couldn't wrap his head around why anyone would choose two wheels over four. "A car is safer," he argued repeatedly, his voice echoing with worry.
He envisioned me in something small and sturdy, like a second-hand Maruti 800, something that would enclose me in metal, something with four wheels for stability.

My mother, on the other hand, was far more concerned with stories of accidents and tragedies. "It's too dangerous," she'd say, her voice trembling with the weight of every story she had ever heard about motorcycle crashes. She had been a witness to numerous bike accidents on the daily soaps running on the television, wherein the accident sometimes took two episodes to conclude and the death was stretched to even more episodes!

For her, even the thought of me on a bike was enough to bring her anxiety bubbling to the surface. The Honda Unicorn wasn't just about convenience—it was about freedom. I needed it, not only to navigate the chaotic streets of Kerala but also to carve out a space for myself in a world that felt too restrictive. Public buses were unreliable at best and crowded to the point of suffocation at worst. I had grown weary of waiting for hours, squeezed between strangers, only to arrive at college tired and frustrated. I craved the freedom to move at my own pace, to ride without being at the mercy of someone else's schedule.

So, I began my campaign, weaving my arguments into every conversation. "It's practical," I said, emphasizing the need to cut down my commute. "The bus takes too long. It's crowded, it's exhausting, and it's not safe at night."

My mother's hesitation began to waver when I mentioned the late-night tuitions. "I'm getting back to hostel so late, and the buses aren't reliable," I explained, capitalizing on her protective instincts. "If I had a bike, I could be home faster, and you wouldn't have to worry about me standing by the road in the dark."

But my father was harder to convince. "We'll get you a car," he said, firm in his belief that four wheels were better than two. "A second-hand car. It's safer, and more respectable."

I was ready for this argument. I had armed myself with facts and figures, studying the advantages of the Honda Unicorn and memorizing the details. "A car is too expensive," I countered. "The maintenance, the fuel costs—it's too much. A bike is economical, and I'll be able to cut through traffic when I'm running late. A car would just slow me down."

And so, the debate raged on. Every evening at the dinner table, I made my case, bit by bit, until I could see their resolve starting to crack. My father, the ever-practical man, began to see the logic in my arguments. My mother, though still afraid, trusted me enough to believe I would be responsible. Finally, after weeks of persistence, they agreed.

"You can get the bike," my father said, his voice tinged with resignation, "but you must promise to be careful. No reckless riding. And you'll need to get proper safety gear."

I agreed eagerly, barely able to contain my excitement. The battle was won.

The day I finally got my Honda Unicorn felt like a dream. The black paint shimmered in the sunlight, and the grey stripes along the fuel tank added a sleek elegance to its muscular form. Standing in front of it, I felt a rush of emotions—excitement, pride, anticipation. This was more than just a bike. It was the culmination of my hard-fought independence.

When I first sat on the seat, I could feel the weight of the bike beneath me—a solid, powerful machine that was now mine. I ran my fingers along the handlebars, savoring the feel of the smooth metal and the firm grip of the rubber. Turning the key in the ignition, I felt a surge of adrenaline as the engine roared to life with a low, steady hum.

The first ride wasn't a wild rush down the highway, as much as I wanted it to be. Instead, I kept it slow and steady, easing my way through the neighbourhood streets, getting a feel of the bike. The monoshock suspension was smooth – way ahead of other bikes in the market that time, absorbing every bump in the road with ease, and the handling was responsive, making me feel like I was gliding rather than riding. As I rode, the wind whipped past me, cool against my skin, carrying with it a sense of freedom I had never experienced before.
For the first time in my life, I was truly free.

Owning a bike wasn't just about riding—it was about learning how to *live* with it. I spent hours in the garage, getting to know my Honda Unicorn, familiarizing myself with its parts and understanding the mechanics that made it run. I learned how to change the oil, adjust the brakes, and check the tire pressure. I wanted to know every inch of the machine, to understand its inner workings as deeply as I understood my own desires for freedom.

But riding wasn't just about the mechanics—it was an art form, one that required patience and skill. The roads in Bengaluru were unpredictable, full of potholes, sudden obstacles, and chaotic traffic. I learned how to navigate through it all, how to balance speed with caution, and how to anticipate the movements of other drivers. Riding wasn't just about getting from point A to point B anymore—it was about mastering the journey.

Every ride was a lesson, and with each one, my confidence grew. I began to push the bike harder, taking it on longer rides, venturing out into the hills and the countryside that surrounded the city. There was a peacefulness in those rides, the way the world seemed to slow down as I moved through it, the landscape changing from the busy streets of the city to the quiet solitude of nature.

The bike became my sanctuary, a place where I could escape the pressures of daily life and lose myself in the rhythm of the road.

With the Honda Unicorn, I had gained more than just a mode of transportation. I had gained independence. I was no longer bound by the erratic schedules of public transportation, no longer dependent on anyone to get me where I needed to go. The bike gave me the freedom to move through the world on my own terms, to explore new places, and to carve out my own path.

It also gave me a newfound sense of confidence. I was no longer the quiet, uncertain teenager who had to ask permission for everything. I was in control—not just of the bike, but of my life. The Honda Unicorn wasn't just a machine—it was a reflection of the person I was becoming strong, independent, and fearless to take on the world.

The Honda Unicorn became a constant companion throughout my college years and beyond. It was there for late-night rides with friends, spontaneous trips to nearby towns, and quiet moments of solitude on the open road. It was more than just a bike—it was a part of me, a symbol of the freedom I had fought so hard to attain.

Looking back, I realize that the bike wasn't just a vehicle—it was a metaphor for the journey I was on. The journey toward independence, the journey toward discovering who I was, and the journey toward carving out my own place in the world. Every ride was a step closer to that goal, a reminder that I had the power to shape my own destiny, no matter how difficult the road ahead might be.

As the years passed, the bike became a symbol of the strength and resilience I had developed along the way. It was a reminder of the battles I had fought, the fears I had overcome, and the freedom I had earned.

The first bike is never just a bike. It's a declaration of independence, a statement of intent, and for me, it was the start of a journey that would continue for years to come.

Cars to Bikes – A Shift in Love

It's strange to think that there was a time when motorcycles didn't captivate me at all. In fact, I was once obsessed with something entirely different: cars. The comfort of being enclosed in a metal shell, the smooth hum of an engine, and the idea of cruising down an open road in a car always seemed so appealing to me.

Before I ever fell in love with bikes, I used to devour car magazines like *Autocar* and *Overdrive*, which fed my passion for the automotive world, reinforcing my belief that cars were the ultimate form of independence. The sleek designs, the innovation in engines, the luxury, and comfort—everything about cars seemed like the ideal blend of freedom and elegance. The movies like Fast & the Furious brought so much attraction towards fast cars, which led me to believe that cars were the pinnacle of freedom. But life, as it often does, took me in a different direction, and the love I once had for cars was slowly eclipsed by a new passion for motorcycles.

This chapter is about that shift—how the thrill of bikes overtook the comfort of cars, how a passion once rooted in sleek sedans and hatchbacks, transformed into something rawer, more visceral, and how these two worlds collided within me, reshaping my sense of freedom.

There was always something about cars that made me feel safe and secure, as if the act of driving enclosed me in a world of my own making. When I first began dreaming of independence, I didn't imagine myself on a motorcycle tearing through busy streets. Instead, I pictured myself behind the wheel of a car, windows down, the gentle breeze brushing my hair, the sound of soft music filling the air.

In many ways, my love for cars was tied to my feminine self, the part of me that craved elegance and grace in everything I did. Cars, especially the ones I would obsess over in *Autocar* and *Overdrive*, were often described with terms that resonated deeply with that side of me— "sleek", "smooth", "luxurious".

Driving a car felt poised, refined, and that idea appealed to the part of me that longed for quiet sophistication. The way a car responded to the slightest touch, the seamless control it offered—it all felt effortless, much like the way I hoped to move through life.

When I was behind the wheel of a car, I didn't have to wrestle with the elements or struggle for control. Instead, I could glide through the streets, shielded from the noise and chaos of the world outside.

That feeling of being enclosed, of being protected, resonated with my desire for a quiet, safe space where I could simply exist without the pressures of the world bearing down on me. I found solace in the way the leather seats cradled me, the way the steering wheel turned smoothly beneath my hands, the way the engine purred quietly beneath the hood. There was no rush, no need for speed—just the gentle rhythm of the road unfolding before me.

For as long as I could remember, cars symbolized freedom, but a kind of freedom that was grounded in stability and control. I devoured every issue of *Autocar* and *Overdrive* I could get my hands on, eagerly reading reviews of the latest sedans, luxury vehicles, and sports cars. These magazines were filled with glossy images of cars, their aerodynamic designs highlighted by soft lighting, their interiors plush and comfortable. Thanks to these magazines and my urge to know more about cars, I had become a local guide to cars for the people in the neighbourhood and my school, later in my college too!

It was easy to fall in love with the way these cars were described, with words like "refined," "sophisticated," and "elegant" jumping off the page. The language surrounding cars appealed to my desire for a life that was smooth and controlled, free from the turbulence of uncertainty.

I remember spending hours leafing through the pages of these magazines, fantasizing about owning a car one day—something practical yet stylish, something that spoke to my love for quiet grace. The cars in those magazines weren't just machines; they were extensions of the people who drove them, reflections of their personalities. And for someone like me, who was still trying to figure out who I was, those cars represented the kind of person I wanted to become—someone in control, someone who moved through life with elegance and ease.

The articles in *Autocar* and *Overdrive* often focused on the latest technology in cars, the innovations that made driving easier, smoother, and more comfortable. They would describe the interior designs in great detail, from the softness of the seats to the advanced infotainment systems. I was drawn to the idea of sitting in a car that felt more like a sanctuary more than a two wheleer.

But as much as I loved the idea of cars, my interest in them was rooted in a desire for comfort and security. I loved the thought of being enclosed in a protective shell, where I didn't have to worry about the chaos of the road or the unpredictability of traffic, which was comparatively lesser than that of a two wheeler.

In a car, I could be in control without having to confront the elements, without having to worry about balance or speed. It was the perfect reflection of the person I was at the time—someone who longed for stability and grace, someone who wasn't quite ready to embrace the unpredictable nature of life.

The shift from cars to bikes wasn't immediate. It began slowly, almost imperceptibly, after my chance encounter with a senior at garage in college. I've already shared how that moment led to my first ride on a motorcycle and how it changed everything for me. But what I haven't yet explored is how that experience began to pull me away from my love for cars and into a new world of speed, freedom, and unfiltered thrill.

At first, I resisted the change. Bikes seemed too rough, too wild for someone like me. I had always associated motorcycles with a certain kind of raw masculinity, something that didn't fit with the elegance and poise I had always admired in cars. Femininity was associated with scooties which were easier to ride, considering the attires worn by women. Where cars were smooth and controlled, bikes were loud, unpredictable, and dangerous. But once I experienced that first ride—once I felt the wind rushing past me, the vibration of the engine beneath me, the way the bike responded to every movement—I couldn't deny that something inside me had shifted.

It wasn't just the thrill of speed that drew me in, though that certainly played a part. It was the sense of connection I felt with the bike, the way it became an extension of my body in a way that a car never could. On a bike, I wasn't enclosed or protected—I was exposed to the elements, vulnerable, but in that vulnerability, I found a new kind of strength. I found a sense of freedom that I hadn't realized I had been missing till then.
Slowly, my love for cars began to fade into the background. It wasn't that I stopped appreciating them—I still admired the grace and beauty of a well-designed car—but my heart was no longer in it. I no longer spent hours poring over car magazines, dreaming of owning a sedan or a sports car. Instead, I found myself gravitating toward motorcycles, reading reviews of the latest models, watching videos of bike races, and immersing myself in a world that I had once dismissed as too rough for me.

The more I rode motorcycles, the more I realized that cars, for all their comfort and elegance, couldn't give me the same sense of freedom. In a car, I was always shielded, protected from the world outside. But on a bike, there was nothing between me and the road. The wind whipped through my hair, the sun beat down on my skin, and the roar of the engine became a steady pulse that drove me forward.

Riding a bike wasn't just about getting from one place to another—it was about the journey itself. It was about feeling every bump in the road, every shift in the wind, every curve in the landscape. It was about being fully present in the moment, completely attuned to the world around me. On a bike, I couldn't hide behind the safety of metal and glass. I had to confront the elements head-on, and in doing so, I found a new kind of freedom.

That freedom wasn't just physical—it was emotional. Riding a bike required me to let go of the need for control, to surrender to the unpredictability of the road. And in that surrender, I found a sense of peace that I had never experienced before. The world became simpler, quieter, more focused. There were no distractions, no unnecessary noise—just me, the bike, and the road stretching out before me.

The shift from cars to bikes wasn't just about a change in passion—it was about a change in perspective. Cars, with their comfort and elegance, had once represented the kind of life I wanted to lead—controlled, stable, and refined. But as I grew older and more confident in myself, I began to realize that life wasn't meant to be lived in a bubble. It was meant to be experienced fully, with all its risks and rewards.

Bikes offered me a kind of freedom that cars never could. They allowed me to embrace the chaos of the road, to let go of the need for control, and to find joy in the unpredictable nature of life. They taught me that freedom isn't about being protected—it's about being open to whatever comes your way.

Now, when I think back on my love for cars, I don't regret it. It was an important part of my journey, a reflection of who I was at the time. But bikes have given me something more—a sense of freedom.

Nurpur & Splendor

It was a breezy afternoon in *Nurpur*, a small, sleepy town nestled in the foothills of Himachal Pradesh. Nurpur wasn't a place that buzzed with the urgency of life like New Delhi, where I had spent most of my years working. It was quiet, peaceful, and the hum of city life had been replaced by the rustling of trees and the faint sounds of cowbells in the distance. It had been four months since I'd moved here, away from the clamor of Delhi, where the cost of living had skyrocketed, making it impossible for someone like me—just a freelance content writer— to thrive. But Nurpur, with its slower pace and simplicity, felt like a long-needed exhale. It allowed me to live a fuller life, one that I didn't have to compress into the crowded, fast-paced demands of a big city.

Nurpur wasn't known for much in the eyes of the world, but to me, it became a sanctuary. The town lay cradled between hills, kissed by the cool mountain breezes that swept through its streets. Every morning, the sun rose gently over the hills, casting a soft golden hue over the terracotta rooftops and whitewashed walls of the houses. It felt like the perfect escape from the concrete jungle of Delhi. Nurpur's streets were often deserted except for the occasional cycle rickshaw or the cows meandering along, undeterred by human presence.

The markets were quaint and intimate. There was a lingering fragrance of dried herbs, flowers, and local Himachali food mixed with the musty smell of earthen pots. There was an unhurried rhythm to life here—people moved about their days without the palpable rush that I had grown accustomed to in the capital. Nurpur's residents were largely warm, curious, and surprisingly welcoming. They didn't seem to mind when I, a transwoman new to the town, settled in their midst. Instead, they greeted me with nods of acceptance, curiosity replaced with a gentle kindness I had never quite experienced before.

Children played cricket in the narrow lanes, their loud laughter echoing through the alleys. The elderly gathered at the town's lone chai shop, sipping tea and exchanging gossip about the day's happenings. The big and luxurious cars of Delhi's big shots were replaced by more practical and economical cars and bikes. These were mere means of transport for the public. As time passed, I found myself weaving into the very fabric of Nurpur's small yet bustling society. Here, I felt anonymous and safe, shielded from the prying eyes of the city. The simplicity of life allowed me to blend in, and I grew comfortable in my skin, in my identity, something that I had struggled with back in Delhi.

I stayed in a quaint *kothi*, part of an urban village-like setup. The Kothi was a middle-class dwelling, over 50 years old, filled with a certain character and history. The white paint was peeling off in some corners, and the windows, framed with old wooden shutters, creaked every time they were opened. The structure was sturdy, with a high-ceilinged living room, an arched entrance, and a sprawling courtyard at the back. The floors were made of cool stone, slightly cracked but always polished to a smooth shine. There were multiple rooms, some occupied by the families that had lived in the area for decades, while others—like mine—were rented out to working women like me. I wonder how the quality of construction in those days is better than what we are getting now!

The *kothi* had a rustic charm. The walls were adorned with fading portraits of the landlord's ancestors, and the musty smell of age lingered in the air, especially after the monsoon rains. Despite the creaking doors and occasional plumbing issues, it had a homey atmosphere. The kitchen had a large stone sink, and there was always the scent of freshly ground spices and simmering dals wafting through the space, reminding me of the sense of community that had formed within these old walls.

I shared one side of the house with three other girls: Aakriti, Bella, and Vineeta. All of us were freelance content writers, working remotely but finding solace in each other's company. We weren't just colleagues—we had become friends, almost like family. The house was always lively, filled with laughter, debates over deadlines, and late-night gossip sessions. The time from 8 PM to 10 PM was a time when the whole house gathered together to have food which was shared amongst all and the dinner wasn't complete without the TV serials on a small CRT TV of the 90s with a broken label of BPL on it. Despite our diverse backgrounds, we shared a unique bond. We were united by our passion for words and the quiet life that Nurpur afforded us.

Moving to Nurpur had marked a significant change in my life, not only in terms of location but in my career as well. Back in Delhi, I had struggled with the cutthroat competitiveness of the freelance world. But here, in the stillness of the hills, I had found my niche as a freelance technical content writer. Writing had always been my refuge—a way to express myself when words failed in person, and now, it had become my livelihood.

I had always enjoyed writing about technical subjects—the intricate balance of logic, analysis, and creativity that came with explaining complex technologies in simple, relatable terms. It was a challenge I relished. I would spend hours researching the latest trends in software development, artificial intelligence, and cloud computing, turning dry technical jargon into engaging narratives for my clients. Every project was like piecing together a puzzle, and there was a deep satisfaction in finding just the right way to explain something complicated in a way that anyone could understand.

As a freelancer, my days were unstructured but fulfilling. I would wake up early, the soft light filtering through the curtains of my room, and make myself a strong cup of coffee before settling down with my laptop in the corner of the living room. The world outside the Kothi would still be quiet at that hour, the only sound the gentle hum of my laptop fan as I typed away, words flowing from my fingertips as I delved into the world of words.

Working remotely also allowed me the creative freedom to explore different writing styles. I wasn't just confined to technical writing—I dabbled into product reviews and even ghostwriting on numerous occasions. Each project was a new adventure, and I loved the variety that came with my work. The flexibility of freelancing suited my new life in Nurpur perfectly. It allowed me to create a balance between work and personal time, something I had struggled to achieve in the fast-paced environment of Delhi.

One of the most profound gifts Nurpur had given me was the deep friendship and unconditional acceptance I had found with the women I lived with. Aakriti, Bella, Vineeta, and I had formed a tight-knit team, not just in our work but in our personal lives as well. They had embraced me wholeheartedly, never once making me feel like I didn't belong or that I was different. For someone who had always felt like an outsider in Delhi, it was a feeling that I cherished deeply.

I had known Aakriti since my college days in Bangalore, long before I had begun my transition. She had been one of my closest confidantes during those years, always offering a listening ear and a kind word when I struggled with my identity.

Aakriti had been there for me through the ups and downs, through the confusion and uncertainty, always offering her unwavering support. It was she who had suggested I move to Nurpur and join their team of freelance writers when I could no longer afford the cost of living in Delhi. It was she who had introduced me to Bella and Vineeta, assuring me that I would find acceptance and friendship with them. And she had been right.

Bella was a firecracker—full of energy, always ready with a witty remark or a sarcastic quip. She wrote primarily for lifestyle blogs and fashion magazines, but she had a deep interest in technology as well, often peppering me with questions about my work. Vineeta was quieter, more introspective, but no less talented. She specialized in academic writing, churning out well-researched papers on subjects ranging from environmental science to philosophy.

Despite our different writing styles and personalities, we had developed a camaraderie that was hard to describe. We supported each other through tough deadlines, late-night rewrites, and the occasional writer's block. Outside of work, we were each other's pillars, offering comfort and laughter when life felt overwhelming.

Aakriti, in particular, was my rock. She had been by my side during some of the most challenging moments of my life, guiding me through my decision to transition, helping me navigate the emotional rollercoaster that came with it. She never once questioned my choices or made me feel like I had to justify myself to her. She was simply there, always with a smile and a word of encouragement, reminding me that I had the right to live my life as the woman I had always known myself to be.

Life in Nurpur had also brought with it a newfound love for *Patiala suits*, a traditional dress worn by many women in Punjab and Himachal Pradesh. It was a common sight in the streets—women wearing brightly coloured Patiala suits with intricately embroidered dupattas, moving gracefully as they went about their day. The suits were not only beautiful, but they were also incredibly comfortable. Loose-fitting, with pleats that gathered at the waist, the Patiala pants allowed for easy movement, while the long, flowing kurta added an air of elegance.
When I first moved to Nurpur, I had been hesitant to wear traditional clothing. I was still adjusting to my new life as a transwoman, and there was always the lingering fear of standing out, of drawing unwanted attention. But as the months went by, I began to feel more at ease.

The more I saw these beautiful, flowing Patiala suits, the more intrigued I became. There was something inherently graceful about them, a softness and elegance that felt very much in tune with the person I was becoming. One day, with encouragement from Aakriti and the others, I decided to try one on. I remember the excitement in their eyes as I walked into the small tailor shop in the heart of Nurpur. The shop was a cozy space, filled with the scent of fresh fabric and the vibrant colours of the suits hanging on the walls. After a few fittings, I chose a bright yellow Patiala suit that I instantly fell in love with. The first time I wore it, I felt a rush of joy. The way the fabric moved with me, the pleats gathering and swaying with each step, made me feel both beautiful and free. There was a sense of belonging that came with wearing traditional attire, a connection to the culture around me. In a way, the Patiala suit had become a part of my identity, a symbol of my acceptance in this small town that had welcomed me so warmly.

One afternoon, while waiting for a manuscript to arrive, I received a call from the local courier office informing me that it needed to be picked up. The office was about 10 kilometres away, and while there were buses available, I felt a sense of hesitation about taking public transport. Although I was slowly growing more comfortable in my identity, I still felt apprehensive about standing out in crowded places.

Coincidentally, Kishan, a young man in his early twenties who often came to the *kothi* for odd jobs, was working on the roof that day. Kishan was respectful and always addressed me as “Didi” with genuine warmth. Seeing my dilemma, I asked him if he would be able to take me to the courier office, knowing he had a bike. However, Kishan explained that he had a lot of work left and wouldn’t finish before sunset. After a moment, he offered an unexpected solution: "Didi, take my bike! It’s right there, ready to go."

At first, I hesitated. I hadn’t ridden a bike since I started living as a woman. But then, Aakriti, who had been listening from the doorway, beamed with excitement. She grabbed the keys and the helmet, practically dragging me toward the bike parked outside. It was a Hero Honda Splendor, black with a slightly faded paint job that hinted at the many miles it had seen. My heart raced as I climbed onto the seat, my yellow Patiala suit flowing gracefully around me. With a deep breath, I turned the key, and as I glanced at Aakriti, I could see her pride shining through. "You’ve got this!" she cheered, her eyes brimming with encouragement.

I hadn’t realized how much I missed the feel of a motorcycle until that very moment. This bike was different from the ones I had ridden in the past, and as I prepared to kick-start it, memories of my old biking days came flooding back.

This Splendor didn't have an electric start, so I kicked down hard, feeling the engine roar to life beneath me. The familiar hum of the engine and the slight vibrations beneath my hands were like reconnecting with an old friend.

The afternoon air was crisp, the scent of pine and mountain soil hanging in the breeze. The gentle warmth of the sun had begun to mellow, and a light wind tousled the loose strands of my hair that peeked out from under the helmet. Taking a deep breath, I eased the bike out of the narrow lane of the *kothi* and onto the main road, feeling an exhilarating sense of freedom wash over me. As I rode through the quiet streets, I could feel people's eyes on me. Some glanced curiously, while others simply admired the sight of someone riding confidently, draped in a bright yellow Patiala suit that fluttered gracefully in the wind.

The ride was more than just a journey to the courier office; it was a reclaiming of a part of myself that I had put aside. Riding a bike had always been about freedom and independence for me, but now, it also symbolized my courage to live my life as a transwoman in this small town, unafraid of who I was or how others saw me. As I sped along the road, I felt the weight of my fears and insecurities begin to lift, replaced by the pure joy of the open road and the wind on my face.

With every turn of the wheels, I found myself slipping back into the old rhythm of riding, but with a newfound appreciation for the journey. People continued to watch as I rode past them, perhaps intrigued by the sight of a woman confidently navigating the roads on a bike in traditional attire. But hidden behind my helmet, I felt a sense of anonymity, a feeling of liberation that allowed me to embrace every aspect of my identity without fear or hesitation.

The road stretched out ahead, lined with tall deodar trees that cast long shadows in the fading afternoon light. The warmth of the sun had settled into a gentle glow, and as I passed fields and farmhouses, I felt a deep connection to my surroundings. There was something about riding that made me feel alive, something that stirred my soul in a way few things could. This ride, this seemingly simple task of picking up a package, had turned into a journey of self-discovery and empowerment.

With each passing mile, I became more aware of the pride I felt—not just in my ability to ride, but in my journey, my resilience, and my newfound love for this peaceful, simple life in Nurpur. The ride was a reminder that while I had changed in many ways, my passion for biking remained as fierce as ever.

Neighbour's Pulsar

My life in Nurpur had a newfound tranquility, with each day unfolding in the quiet charm of this small town. Here, nestled among rolling hills and vast landscapes, my world had shifted away from the rush and noise of Delhi. The air was always cool, and the town felt untouched, with its little winding streets, hillside views, and the warmth of its people. Moving here had given me space to rediscover myself. Freelance writing from my corner of the old *kothi* felt more like a gift than a job; the tranquil pace of this town allowed my creativity to bloom.

The *kothi* where I stayed was a charming, rustic building, more like a character from an old book than a mere residence. Its thick, timeworn walls spoke of history, with peeling paint revealing layers of memories from decades past. There were four of us women here: Aakriti, Bella, Vineeta, and me. We each had our own space, but the common areas and terrace became gathering points where laughter and stories filled the air. Kishan's Hero Honda Splendor had become my unexpected companion in this new life. Kishan, a kind-hearted young man who worked odd jobs around the town, had a simple, unassuming way about him. He'd swing by our *kothi* frequently, often to handle maintenance or repairs.

He respected my presence and always referred to me as "Didi." Over time, borrowing his bike had become a tradition. He'd simply hand over the keys with a grin and a gentle "Didi, ride safe". The Splendor wasn't a powerhouse, but it had charm—a gentle purr, a reliable hum that felt like a steady friend.

Every time I took the Splendor out, a part of me reconnected with the biker I used to be, a part of myself I thought I had left behind. The familiar grip of the handles, the slight jolt of the engine—it all grounded me in the present moment. And in these moments, Nurpur felt even more like home, as if the town and the bike had accepted me just as I was.

Anil was one of those rare souls who could instantly brighten any room with his infectious smile and boundless energy. A college student in his late teens, he often visited me on the terrace, drawn perhaps by a mixture of curiosity and admiration. He took to calling me *"Didi jaan,"* a term that rang with playful affection. We'd often cross paths on the terrace, where I'd go to dry the laundry or prepare pickles, a skill I'd picked up in Nurpur. These moments were our time together, spaces filled with laughter, stories, and conversations about life.

Anil poured his heart out during these talks. From his struggles at college to his crushes, his dreams, and, most importantly, his desire to own a bike, he shared it all. His deepest longing was to own a Bajaj Pulsar 220, a powerful machine he believed would make him feel invincible on the road. Whenever he spoke about it, his face would light up with excitement. But the only thing standing in his way was his parents' reluctance. They saw the bike as a potential danger, especially for someone young and inexperienced.

Anil knew his parents respected me, and so he asked me to speak to them on his behalf.

"Didi jaan, they listen to you. If you talk to them, they'll understand," he said, his gaze earnest.

Himachal has a deep respect for transwomen, and with my education and work as a writer, I had gained an additional layer of acceptance here in Nurpur. The community treated me with respect, often inviting me to their homes during celebrations and special occasions. With Anil's request, I felt a gentle responsibility to help him and bridge this gap between him and his parents.

When I arrived at Anil's home to talk to his parents, I was greeted with warmth, a sign of the deep respect they held for me. We settled in their modest yet welcoming living room, where the aroma of fresh chai wafted from the kitchen. Anil's father, a quiet man with a serious gaze, sat across from me, his attention focused. His mother, hands folded neatly in her lap, offered a small smile, though her worry for her son was evident.

I began the conversation gently, acknowledging their concerns while emphasizing Anil's maturity.

"He's a good boy," I said, "and having this bike could be a way for him to learn responsibility." His father listened thoughtfully, nodding occasionally.

I spoke about how the bike could help Anil grow, how it could be a tool for teaching discipline, accountability, and independence.

I assured them, "I'll make sure he rides responsibly, and I'll guide him through it. You have my word." His mother's face softened, and her eyes flickered with understanding as she looked at her son, seated quietly by her side.

Finally, his father gave a nod, his voice a mix of caution and love. "If you're willing to help him, then we'll support him," he said, and I could see Anil's eyes light up with gratitude.

This wasn't just a moment of victory for him; it was a moment of trust and connection, one that would solidify our bond as family in the truest sense.

A few days later, Anil arrived at the *kothi* with a radiant grin, a box of *besan ke laddoo* in his hands. "Didi jaan, these are for you," he said, beaming with pride as he offered me the sweets.

The joy in his eyes was infectious, and as we shared the sweets on the terrace, he thanked me repeatedly, his gratitude spilling over into every word. As the sun dipped below the hills, casting the terrace in a soft golden glow, I spoke to Anil about responsibility. "Owning a bike is a privilege, Anil," I said gently. "It's not just a machine; it's a reminder that you have to be accountable—for yourself, for your family's trust, and for everyone on the road." He listened intently, his usual playful demeanor replaced by a rare seriousness.

"You're the young man of the house now," I continued, placing a hand on his shoulder. "With this bike, you're taking on a new role, a role that requires maturity and respect. Study well, stay true to your values, and remember that we're all here for you. Mistakes are part of life, but it's what you learn from them that counts." Anil nodded, his gaze thoughtful, and I could see that my words had reached him. Our conversation felt like a rite of passage, a gentle push into the world of adulthood, and I felt grateful to be part of his journey.

A week later, Anil surprised me with an offer. “Didi jaan, take the Pulsar for a ride,” he urged, holding out the keys with a wide grin. I hesitated, my fingers brushing against the sleek, polished keys in his hand. The Pulsar was different from Kishan’s Splendor—stronger, faster, and more powerful. I looked down at myself, clad in a black satin Patiala suit, my *dupatta* draped loosely around my neck. The fabric flowed softly with every movement, and I felt an unexpected confidence blooming within me.

Taking a deep breath, I slipped on the helmet, securing the strap under my chin. The bike’s seat felt solid beneath me, the handlebars cool to the touch. I turned the key, and the engine roared to life with a deep, powerful hum. As I shifted into the first gear and rolled out of the *kothi*, I felt a surge of adrenaline, the familiar thrill of biking coursing through my veins.

The day was perfect for a ride—the sky a brilliant blue, the air crisp and clear. The bike responded to every movement, every shift in weight, as if it were an extension of myself. Riding through Nurpur, I could feel people’s eyes on me, some curious, others admiring. But hidden beneath the helmet, I felt anonymous, free to be myself without the weight of anyone’s gaze. I looked into the rear view mirror and the first thing I noticed was my lips covered in a maroon shade lipstick and my head under a half face helmet. I smiled back at the mirror, adjusted the rear view and throttled!

With each turn, each stretch of road, I felt the world open up around me, the hills and valleys unfolding like a story waiting to be told. My *dupatta* fluttered behind me, a ribbon of black against the vivid landscape, and I felt an overwhelming sense of peace. The Pulsar's power was intoxicating, the hum of the engine a steady pulse that matched the rhythm of my heartbeat. It was as if the road itself was calling me, urging me to rediscover the joy of biking, a joy I had once thought I'd left behind. Returning to the *kothi*, I handed the keys back to Anil with a smile, but I knew something had shifted within me. This wasn't just a ride—it was a reminder, a rekindling of a love I thought I had lost. Over the past months, riding Kishan's Splendor had brought me a sense of comfort, a steady connection to the open road, but riding this Pulsar felt different. More power, more style and more confidence to push myself.

As I rolled the Pulsar 220 back into the courtyard of the *kothi* and handed the keys to Anil, a sense of lingering exhilaration stayed with me. This wasn't just a simple ride to test a bike—it had rekindled a connection within me, a part of myself I had thought I'd left in the past. Riding had once been a way for me to escape, to feel a sense of control and freedom. Now, it was a way to reconnect with that freedom, but in a different light. I wasn't the same person I'd been before transitioning, before leaving the city, or before re-discovering my life in Nurpur.

The months of riding Kishan's Splendor had shown me that the passion for biking was still alive within me, though it had taken on new forms. Each ride, each moment on the road, brought me closer to understanding that biking was as much a part of my life as writing, as my new identity, as my newfound friendships. Aakriti, sensing my excitement, listened with rapt attention that evening as I shared my thoughts. "Maybe biking is calling you back, Naina," she said, her voice thoughtful yet encouraging. "It's always been more than just a way to get around for you."

She was right; biking wasn't just a mode of transport. It was an expression of freedom, a means to explore both the world and me, a way to live in the moment. This realization made me smile as I remembered the looks of admiration, curiosity, and acceptance I'd received that day on the Pulsar. The journey back to biking was already happening, with each ride weaving a story that felt uniquely my own.

Chotti Chotti Khushiyaan

Nurpur wasn't just a town; it was a place where I could learn to breathe again. With its quaint little lanes shaded by old trees, the laughter of children playing in the streets, and neighbors who took the time to greet each other, it felt like stepping back into a gentler world. Life moved at a slower pace here, each day unfolding softly, giving me the space to build a life on my own terms.

The *kothi* I shared with Aakriti, Bella, and Vineeta felt like a haven. Aakriti would begin her day with yoga, contorting herself into poses I couldn't imagine attempting, while Bella would settle in with a mug of coffee, offering commentary on everything from the news to the latest village gossip. Vineeta, the quietest among us, often had her nose in a book, surfacing only to offer a wise word or two. Each of these women added a richness to my life in Nurpur, bringing laughter, support, and a sense of belonging.

One day, I caught Bella watching me as I practiced walking around the living room, holding my head high, shoulders relaxed, trying to walk with the same ease and grace the women around me seemed to have. She burst into laughter. "Naina, are you trying to become a Bollywood heroine or something?"

I blushed, grinning back. "Just practicing. It's a work in progress!"

She raised her mug in a mock salute, her eyes twinkling. “You’re getting there. Keep at it, and soon you’ll be outshining all of us!” The laughter that followed was warm, the kind that only true friends can share.

Learning to carry myself as a woman wasn’t as simple as slipping into a *salwar kameez*. It was a process that involved unlearning years of habits and mannerisms. I spent hours practicing how to walk with softer steps, adjusting the angle of my chin, and even finding ways to let my hands rest gently on my lap, as I’d noticed the women here do. But the most challenging part was modulating my voice. I wanted to speak with a softer tone, so I’d practice in front of the mirror, whispering phrases to myself, then gradually adding volume. It was during these practices that Aakriti found me one evening, amused by my efforts. “Practicing your princess voice?” she teased.

I laughed, letting her in on my struggles. “Yes! But it’s harder than it looks.”

Together, we’d mimic the way the women in Nurpur spoke, with a rhythm that was both musical and gentle. Soon, Bella and Vineeta joined in, and these practice sessions turned into moments filled with giggles and exaggerated attempts at sounding posh. Through these conversations, they taught me how to carry myself in different social settings, each correction they offered coming with a smile or a playful nudge.

Cooking and cleaning around the *kothi* became unexpected moments of growth. Anil's mother would join us sometimes, teaching us old family recipes and sharing stories. She was the one who insisted that I wear a *dupatta* while cooking, explaining, "It's part of the tradition, Naina. A woman's *dupatta* is her crown."

In these simple tasks, I learned about poise, humility, and strength. Each fold in the dough we made, each vegetable we chopped, became an exercise in learning the ways of the women around me. They didn't just see me as a student; they saw me as one of their own, guiding me with patience, humor, and warmth. Every compliment they gave, every small correction, felt like an affirmation, a gentle reminder that I was indeed stepping into my identity with pride.

My visit to Rupi Ladies Tailor was a highlight in my Nurpur life. It was a small, busy shop with shelves stacked high with vibrant fabrics and rolls of thread in every color imaginable. Subhash bhaiya, the tailor and my newfound fashion advisor, treated each garment like a work of art. From the moment I stepped in, he treated me with kindness and respect, as if he understood the significance of each piece of clothing in my journey.

One day, while picking out fabric for a new *salwar kameez*, Subhash bhaiya noticed my hesitation as I debated between a deep red and a soft green. "Naina ji," he said thoughtfully, "each fabric has its own story. You have to feel it, see what it speaks to you."
He began introducing me to the world of fabrics and cuts. There was cotton, he explained, perfect for the sweltering heat of Nurpur's summer, comfortable and breathable. Silk was for occasions, for celebrations that needed a touch of luxury. And then there was chiffon, delicate and airy, a fabric that he said matched "a gentle spirit."
"Every fabric," he mused, "brings out a different side of you. Silk is regal, while cotton is humble. Chiffon? Well, that's for when you're feeling a little mischievous." His words filled the small shop with laughter, and I found myself immersed not only in the garments but in their stories, each fabric choice a piece of my evolving identity.

Through Subhash bhaiya's guidance, I learned more than just fashion—I learned self-expression. He would make small suggestions—a slit here, a neckline adjustment there, depth at the back, a zipper at the back—that transformed each outfit into something unique, something I wore with pride. Each outfit became an extension of myself, a reflection of the confidence that was blossoming within me.

Another place that is vividly attached to my memory is the Kali Mata Temple. The Mata temple was a short walk from the *kothi*, a modest building surrounded by marigold garlands and whitewashed walls. Its quiet simplicity held a power that drew people from across the village. The temple's central idol, a statue of the Mata, was captivating—a figure carved in serene beauty, with eyes that seemed to look right into your soul. Her expression was one of strength tempered by compassion, a balance that resonated deeply within me.

People would come to the temple to seek blessings, whispering their wishes and tying small red threads to the ancient tree outside, a ritual of hope. Belief in the Mata's powers ran deep in Nurpur; locals credited her with everything from good harvests to personal healings. Standing before her, I too felt an unexplainable strength, as if I were in the presence of a force that understood every secret, every unspoken wish in my heart.

The temple priest, an elderly man with a gentle smile and eyes that radiated warmth, would often hand me *prasad*—a small blessing in the form of sweets. He never said much, but his silent understanding offered me comfort. In his kind eyes, I saw acceptance. His smile was one that carried the weight of countless blessings, and each time he handed me a piece of *prasad*, I felt a sense of peace settle over me, as if he were telling me, without words, that I was on the right path.

These visits became my moments of grounding. In the temple's silence, surrounded by the soft hum of prayers and the flickering of diyas, I could let go of my worries. The Mata's presence, the acceptance from the priest, and the quiet devotion of the people around me helped me find strength in my own journey. It was a place of refuge, a reminder that, no matter the challenges, there was a force greater than myself guiding me.

One rainy evening, while going through an old drawer, I stumbled upon a stack of photographs. As I flipped through them, a familiar face smiled back at me from a past life—me, standing with my first bike, hair tousled and face filled with a sense of invincibility. I remembered the thrill of those days, the rush of speed, the sense of unbridled freedom that came with riding down open roads. Each picture captured moments of pure joy, memories of a time when I felt as if the world was mine to conquer.

Back then, I was fearless. The world felt limitless as I rode through misty hills, the engine's light grunt echoing in my ears, leaving behind any worries or self-doubt. Now, those rides felt like a different era, a time when freedom came without hesitation. As I looked at the pictures, a pang of longing settled in my chest—a longing for the freedom, the independence that I now had to consider carefully.

In Nurpur, I found that happiness wasn't about dramatic transformations but about embracing the *chotti chotti khushiyaan*, the tiny joys that filled my days with purpose. The smiles exchanged at the market, the soft glow of the evening sun over the hills, and the warmth of my friends in the *kothi*—these small things became the backbone of my new life, the stepping stones guiding me forward.

One particular evening comes to mind: Aakriti, Bella, Vineeta, and I were sitting on the terrace, wrapped in blankets as the night settled over us, sipping on warm chai. Aakriti was regaling us with stories of her dance nights in Bangalore, punctuating her tales with dramatic hand gestures and bursts of laughter. "And then, this one guy thought he could out-dance me!" she exclaimed, nearly spilling her tea. We all laughed, the kind of laughter that fills the air and settles into your heart. When it was my turn to share, I hesitated before saying, "You know, I miss the freedom of riding my bike, of being out on the open road without a single worry."

Bella nodded, her expression soft. "That spirit of adventure is still in you, Naina. It's just… transforming. Like you are." Her words felt like a warm hug, a reminder that the core of who I was—the adventurous spirit, the fearless rider—was still within me, even if expressed differently now.

As I sat there under the starlit sky, surrounded by friends who felt like family, I realized that my journey wasn't about leaving the past behind. It was about weaving the memories of who I was with the woman I was becoming. Yes, there were challenges, boundaries I had to navigate that I hadn't faced before, but there was also a strength growing within me, a strength borne from love, acceptance, and the small joys that Nurpur had offered.

The memories of my past self weren't just nostalgia—they were a testament to my resilience, a reminder of the courage it took to pursue my truth. As I gazed out over the hills, breathing in the night air, I knew that this journey was far from over. The road ahead would continue to offer challenges, but with each *chotti khushi*, each shared smile and silent blessing, I felt more prepared to face whatever lay ahead and with that, I closed my eyes, a quiet smile on my lips, feeling truly at peace. In Nurpur, among friends, laughter, and the gentle strength of the Mata temple, I was finally home.

The Road Less Travelled

Ladakh, which I did in 2014, was my ultimate dream destination, just like every biker. It wasn't just a place on a map—it was a test of will and a journey into solitude. The trip was born out of dreams, plans, efforts and above all, the belief that I could do it. The path ahead was challenging, winding up the mountains, with my reliable Honda Unicorn carrying me over loose gravel, steep inclines and crossing water bodies at fixed places. Each turn revealed a landscape that was both fierce and beautiful, like a beast waiting to be tamed.

The higher I went, the fewer travellers I saw, until it was just me and the mountain's silence. Stopping near Drass one evening, I set up my small camp and looked at the stars scattered across the night sky. There, beneath the vast, indifferent sky, I felt a quiet kind of acceptance. I took out a scarf from my saddlebags and let it drape around my head and shoulders. For a moment, I imagined myself as the woman I longed to be, without fear or hiding. In that quiet solitude, the mountains became silent witnesses to my vulnerability, and I felt a flicker of peace, as if they were urging me to be unafraid of who I was becoming.

Ladakh gave me lot of peace and equivalent amount of memories. Talking to the monks, I realised a lot of things about life that I had never thought about. The things that should have never mattered to me had been prioritised by me so far in life. It was a wake up call for me.

Another big destination was Sikkim that I had been eyeing since college and realised in 2015. The Eastern part of the country was something that I hadn't touched much except a visit to Shillong, Mawsinram and Cherapunjee long back during my college days, travelling by train and buses. This time it was different. The journey to Siliguri was a colourful one as I was on my bike, winding through states and landscapes, each with its own charm and quirks. By this time, I was on my second-hand Karizma, a bike with a fierceness that matched the thrill of adventure I sought. Riding through the plains of Uttar Pradesh and the sprawling fields of Bihar, I felt the pulse of India's heartland.

In Siliguri, I met a solo woman traveler at a chai stall. Her name was Amrita, and she was from Kolkata, carrying the warmth of her city in her open, accepting smile. "Where are you headed?" she asked, her curiosity evident.
"Sikkim," I replied, and then, surprising myself, I added, "You know, sometimes I feel like I'm traveling to find pieces of myself. Like there's a part of me that I haven't fully embraced." She looked at me thoughtfully, sensing there was more to the story.

As the conversation flowed, I found myself opening up about my desire to transition, about the woman I dreamed of being. Amrita didn't flinch; instead, she placed a gentle hand on mine and said, "You're braver than most people for being true to yourself. Moreover, with the facial features that you have, I am sure you will make a beautiful lady one day. Do remember, sometimes, the road we're meant to take is the one that leads us inward". Those words remain etched in me till date.

Her kindness stayed with me, adding a layer of strength and understanding that I carried forward. Later that evening, I treated myself to an experience I had dreamed about—a transformation at a salon named Beautonica in one of the local malls. The staff, enthusiastic and warm, dolled me up in a flowing georgette saree, with a blouse that hugged my frame just right and matching jewellery that added a sparkle to my reflection. Stepping out of the salon as a young woman, I felt an exhilaration I'd never known before. I took an auto around Siliguri that evening, feeling the wind in my hair, my saree flowing, and the city lights dancing around me. The auto driver, polite and respectful, addressed me as "Madam," and each time I heard it, my heart soared. I felt seen, recognized as who I truly was, and that night in Siliguri, I was no longer hiding—I was free.

Next I was headed to Sikkim, crossing Darjeeling and Indo-Nepal border enroute. At the Indo-Nepal border, with the help of my Aadhar card and an entry in the border register at the post manned by the local Police, I was allowed to venture into Nepal up to a few kilometres. I decided to walk and checked out the market. I found a shop with some local clothes but didn't have the courage to go and buy them. I bought some small souvenirs and head back to my bike that was parked around 2 kilometres from me, in India!

The road to Sikkim was one of my most treasured routes. Riding through tea gardens astride the roads in West Bengal, mist-laden valleys, and cascading waterfalls felt like a journey into my own soul. The deeper I went, the more Sikkim's peace seeped into me, helping me feel closer to the person I aspired to be.

During my time in Gangtok, I visited a monastery high in the mountains, where the calm was almost surreal. Inside, crimson-robed monks chanted prayers, filling the air with a rhythm that seemed to reach my very core. There, I met Sonam, a woman from Darjeeling, who had come seeking blessings. We shared a quiet conversation about life's unexpected turns, and again, I found myself sharing my truth.

"I've always felt... different," I confessed, surprised at my own openness. Sonam smiled, her eyes soft with understanding. "Sometimes, the journey isn't about finding who we are, but letting go of who we're not," she said. Her words were like a balm, gentle yet affirming, helping me shed a bit more of the weight I carried.

The monks' chants felt like they were blessing my journey, filling me with a sense of acceptance and peace. That night, wrapped in my scarf as I looked out at the mountains, I felt like Sikkim was giving me permission to embrace my own spirit, flaws and all.

The journey to Shimla in 2013 was a familiar one, yet it felt different each time I rode through the cool mountain roads, past pine forests and quaint dhabas. This time, I rode on my Unicorn, my old friend that carried me as reliably as ever.

Halfway through, near Solan, I stopped at a dhaba run by a woman named Prema. She was busy serving steaming plates of *parathas* and glasses of chai to travellers, and she greeted me with a warm smile. I had forgotten to remove the nail paint from my fingers and didn't even realise it. Prema noticed the maroon nail paint and her eyes grew larger! Her face had questions that she was probably afraid of asking.

She seemed to be a in her early 20s and probably hadn't seen a guy wearing nail paint so far. As she came back with a plate of Maggi noodles, I gave her a gentle smile and asked her about the present condition of the road ahead. She replied "With that nail paint, you can cross any road"! I was surprised and suddenly realised that I hadn't removed the nail paint. For a moment I was embarrassed. She probably noticed that and came back to my table. She said "Bhaiya, sorry if I said something wrong. I didn't want to hurt you". She could now see the woman hiding in me. She came back with a chocolate and gifted it to me, wishing me luck for the road ahead. I thanked her and as I left, she said "The road is a teacher. It teaches us strength, patience, and sometimes, it even teaches us who we are. Take care Didi".

I took her words to heart as I continued my journey to Shimla. Upon reaching, I found myself once again drawn to the winding streets of Mall Road, bustling with families, tourists, and travellers. In the privacy of my guesthouse room, I pulled out my femme clothes and put them on, feeling the fabric wrap around me like an affirmation. I dreamed of walking through Mall Road as a woman, blending in with the crowd, unafraid of being seen. The gentle mountain breeze whispered through the window, and in that small room, I felt Shimla's quiet encouragement, as if it too wished for my freedom.

The next destination from Shimla was Palampur which was known for its tranquillity, and as I rode through the lush green fields on my Unicorn, I felt a deep sense of calm. There was a softness in the air here, a sense of timelessness that made me feel like I could finally pause and breathe. At a roadside stall, I met Meera, a tea plantation worker who sold freshly plucked tea leaves. She offered me a small cup of her brew, and as we sipped, we exchanged stories. Meera, with her expressive eyes and contagious laugh, seemed genuinely interested in my journey.
"There's so much beauty in the way you speak about yourself," she said, after I confessed my inner struggles. "The world may not understand right away, but that doesn't mean you stop being who you are."

Her words stayed with me as I wandered through the tea gardens. Palampur taught me patience, reminding me that just like tea leaves need time to brew, growth and self-acceptance took their own time. Walking through the fields, surrounded by nature's quiet beauty, I realized that some parts of my journey would require gentleness and patience.

The route from Palampur to Manali was thrilling, filled with twists and turns that kept my heart racing. On the Unicorn, I felt an invincible kind of energy, as if the road and I were partners in a dance. The path wound higher into the mountains, the air getting crisper, the world feeling wilder with each mile.

I hit a rough patch when my bike's engine began to sputter. I had foolishly forgotten to check the oil level, and I found myself stranded on a winding mountain path. Fortunately, a local mechanic passed by and helped me fix it, chuckling, "Always respect the mountain and your machine, bhai saab. They both need care."

Reaching Manali felt like a victory. I parked by the Beas River, watching the sun dip below the mountains, casting a golden glow on the water. In that stillness, I wrapped a shawl around myself, feeling the thrill of accomplishment. The mountains, fierce and unyielding, seemed to reflect my own spirit, reminding me that I could overcome even the toughest challenges.

McLeodganj had always felt like a safe harbour for wanderers, seekers, and travellers from across the world. Nestled in the shadow of the Himalayas, the town had a kind of magic in its air—a mix of spirituality and quiet liberation. I had come here seeking solitude and reflection, but I had found something even better: a connection with strangers who would become momentary anchors in my journey. One of those strangers was Sarah.

Sarah was a striking woman from Israel, with piercing blue eyes that seemed to carry the weight of many journeys. She was staying at the same small hotel as I was, and we kept bumping into each other at breakfasts or in the lobby, exchanging polite nods and occasional small talk.

Her presence was hard to miss; there was something effortlessly magnetic about her. We exchanged stories about our travels in brief conversations, but something in her smile told me she was open to deeper conversations. Yet, I was shy—guarded even—and so, I kept our interactions light.

It was the second night at the hotel, and I found myself overcome by a familiar longing. After a quiet dinner, I returned to my room, feeling the thrill of transforming into my true self, a ritual that had become my solace on the road. I put on delicate lingerie, a flowing, floral frock, carefully applied my makeup, and adjusted the wig that cascaded in gentle waves down my shoulders. Tonight, I was going to indulge in a bit of celebration. I opened a cold bottle of beer ignoring the cold weather outside, took a long, refreshing sip, and headed to the balcony with my earphones in. The music carried me away, a soft melody that matched the quiet beauty of the night sky.

The stars hung low, shimmering as if they were close enough to touch. I felt wrapped in a cocoon of calm, swaying gently to the music, entirely lost in the moment. As I gazed at the sky, dreaming of a world where I could live as this woman without hiding, I felt a warm, affirming glow. The beer, the music, the night—they had a way of drawing out this version of me, one that I cherished but rarely shared. Suddenly, I felt a presence. A soft shift in the air. I turned, and there she was: Sarah, standing in her own balcony, separated by a thin wooden divider. She was watching me, her eyes soft and amused, a gentle smile playing on her lips. She waved, and I felt a rush of embarrassment as I removed my earphones. How long had she been standing there?

“You look beautiful,” she said, her voice carrying over like a warm breeze. I felt my cheeks flush, caught between the joy of being seen and the vulnerability of being exposed.

“Thank you,” I stammered, unsure whether to retreat or to stay.

“Don’t be shy,” she laughed lightly. “I’d love to get to know the beautiful girl I’ve been sharing a wall with. Come over! I could use some company,” she invited, her voice sincere, warm. I hesitated only for a moment before making my way over, heart racing with anticipation.

Sarah’s room was cozy, filled with trinkets from her travels—a woven shawl draped over the bed, small clay figures, and colourful postcards. She had been in that room since the past one month and was planning to stay there for a month more. She offered me a seat on the plush chair near the window, and as I settled in, I felt an unspoken ease wash over me, as if this were exactly where I was meant to be.

“I’ll get us something to drink,” she said, pouring two glasses of wine. She handed me one, her gaze steady, full of curiosity but free of judgment. As we sipped, we fell into easy conversation. Sarah spoke about her life in Israel, the mountains she had trekked, and the people she had met. She had a nomadic spirit, wandering wherever the wind called, a bit like me.

Eventually, the conversation turned to me. She sensed there was more to my story and encouraged me to share. I felt a flutter of nervousness, but her presence was like a warm embrace, reassuring me that I could trust her. I took a deep breath and began, sharing how I often felt out of place, how I travelled to explore not just the world but myself.

“I feel like there’s a woman within me,” I confessed, surprised at how easily the words slipped out. “A part of me that’s been waiting to be seen. But it’s not always easy to show her.”

Sarah reached out, placing a comforting hand on mine. “You are that woman. Whether you’re wearing a saree, a frock, pants or anything else, she’s always there. And tonight, she’s sitting right here with me”.

Her words sank into me, a gentle affirmation that resonated in my heart. We talked late into the night, and at some point, she asked me if I’d like to try on some of her clothes. The suggestion brought out an almost childlike excitement within me, and I nodded eagerly.

Sarah brought out a collection of beautiful scarves, dresses, and delicate jewellery, handing me pieces with a glint in her eye. She selected a simple yet elegant dress for me, her hands brushing my shoulders as she helped me slip into it. “This colour suits you,” she murmured, brushing a stray lock of my wig into place. She even took out a makeup kit and offered to brush my cheeks with a hint of blush. I felt like a doll in her hands, cherished and accepted. As she brushed my hair and adjusted the hem of my dress, I couldn’t help but feel an overwhelming sense of joy. It was like a dream—having someone see me, truly see me, and embrace me without hesitation. For once, I felt like the girl I always longed to be, and Sarah was the friend who allowed me to revel in that identity.

“You know, I never had a sister,” Sarah said, smiling as she brushed a final stroke of blush onto my cheeks. “But tonight, I feel like I do.”

I felt tears prick my eyes at her words, and I squeezed her hand in gratitude. “Thank you,” I whispered, my voice catching. “This means more to me than I can say.”

As the night deepened, we moved back to the balcony, two souls wrapped in the shared silence of acceptance. We sat there, looking up at the starlit sky, occasionally laughing at each other's stories and letting the comfort of companionship fill the quiet. In that simple yet profound moment, I felt a sense of liberation I had rarely known. The moonlight danced off our glasses, the distant hum of the town settling into sleep as we shared our stories, fears, and dreams.

As the dawn lightened the sky, Sarah leaned over and said softly, "Remember, Naina, the world is big, but it's also full of people like me who see you, who believe in you. Don't hide that light of yours. You're a beautiful woman—never forget that". Those words, simple and sincere, touched a part of me I had kept hidden for so long. That night with Sarah became one of my most cherished memories, a moment when the road I travelled didn't just lead me somewhere; it led me back to myself. My time with Sarah became a reminder of the strength that came from connection, from opening up to those who were willing to listen and see me for who I truly was.

Each journey I undertook, each stranger I met along the way, added another layer to my understanding of myself. I would go on to face many more miles, countless crossroads, but that night in McLeodganj was a turning point. Sarah's acceptance had given me a glimpse of the woman I was becoming, a reminder that one day, I could walk through the world as her, without fear or reservation and all this happened just because of my love for riding bikes and exploring places through bike trips. I left McLeodganj with a heart full of gratitude, knowing that the journey was far from over, but that with every step, I was getting closer to embracing all that I was.

The destinations and the roads leading to them, from the rugged landscapes of Ladakh to the tea-scented air of Palampur, left an imprint on my heart, pushing me closer to embracing my true self. The roads I travelled were more than pathways between destinations; they became mirrors, reflecting parts of me I was only beginning to understand. In each stretch of silence, every hum of the engine, and each connection with a fellow traveller, I found fragments of the woman I knew myself to be.

The Bypass

The period from 2019 to 2023 was a whirlwind, a time of relentless ambition, growth, and transformation. It was a time when I became so engrossed in chasing my goals that I didn't realize I had neglected the passions that once defined me, like biking. But my journey during these years, filled with a variety of experiences—writing, pageantry, modelling, fitness, and aviation—unveiled different aspects of my personality and pushed me to become someone I had only dreamed of. I was driven by a need to achieve, to be seen, and to make a mark, not just for myself, but for the entire LGBTQ+ community.

The initial years of my career in my new life were spent as a content writer, and it was more than just a job; it was a way to feed my love for automobiles and technology. I found joy in writing articles about engines, bikes, and mechanical systems, and I could feel my fascination for all things mechanical, cultivated since childhood, blossoming through my work. There was something poetic about the precision of engineering—the way metal and machinery came together to form a coherent, powerful entity.

Every article I wrote was an exploration of this world I adored. I would dive into the intricate details of how an engine worked, break down the mechanics of new technologies in automobiles, and write passionately about upcoming innovations. It felt like I was a part of this world even though I wasn't physically working with the machines. My words brought to life the hum of an engine, the thrill of acceleration, and the allure of finely crafted machines.

I worked with clients from the automobile industry, penned blogs and technical articles. It wasn't just about writing; it was about storytelling. I was telling the story of machines, of people's dreams woven with speed and power, of the thrill of the open road that I had known so well. Writing for the automobile sector wasn't just work for me; it was my way of staying connected to the mechanical passions that had shaped my younger days.

As time went on, I transitioned into ghostwriting, a role that allowed me to explore a different facet of my writing talent. Here, my words were no longer attributed to me, but to those who paid for them. I took on projects ranging from technical reports to memoirs, white papers to scripts. There was a certain irony in ghostwriting—lending my voice to others, helping them tell their stories while I stayed in the background.

Writing technical documents and reports for companies helped me understand various industries more deeply, but the creative projects were the ones that stirred my soul. Sometimes I would write scripts for promotional videos or complete unfinished manuscripts for clients, adding depth, flair, and value to the work. The satisfaction lay not in seeing my name in print but in knowing that my words had breathed life into someone else's vision.

During this phase, I often found myself questioning the boundaries of identity. If my words could belong to someone else, who was I, really? Was I just a vessel for ideas and stories, or did I have my own story that was waiting to be told? The answer was not clear, but the questions fuelled my desire to find out.

Pageantry had always intrigued me. The idea of walking the ramp, dressed in beautiful outfits, adorned with elegance, and being admired for grace and beauty was something I had quietly yearned for. It wasn't just about looking pretty; it was about feeling seen and validated. It was about celebrating femininity and claiming a space that had often felt forbidden to me.

My first step into the world of pageantry was a virtual saree contest held during the lockdown—a small online event, but it was significant for me. I wore my finest saree, draped elegantly, and recorded a video of my walk. I was nervous but thrilled; it felt like the world could finally see me, the real me. To my surprise, I won a title in the contest, and the experience lit a fire within me, making me crave the real stage.

The opportunity came with an LGBTQ+ pageant in Mumbai. I walked into it with both excitement and apprehension, but once I took that first step onto the runway, all my fears melted away. Wearing a dazzling gown that hugged my curves just right, I walked with a confidence that came not just from hours of practice, but from years of dreaming. It wasn't just a walk; it was a declaration of who I was.

During the question-answer segment, I spoke about my journey and the importance of representation in the mainstream. I saw the nods of approval in the audience, felt the applause in my bones—it wasn't just my beauty being celebrated, but my courage. I walked away with a sub title, a newfound sense of pride and won many hearts!

After the pageant, I had a few opportunities to model for some brands, mostly low-profile gigs, but they were enough to give me a taste of the world of modelling. I posed for photographers, flaunting sarees and elegant dresses, and for the first time, I saw myself as beautiful, confident, and truly feminine. Finally, I realised that modelling and pageantry were no my cup of tea!

In 2023, I decided it was time to tell my own story to the world in the form of a book. I had spent years writing for others, telling their stories, and now, I felt a deep need to share my own. I poured my experiences into a memoir, recounting the struggles, the victories, the moments of despair, and the flashes of triumph. Writing the book was cathartic, almost like peeling away layers of my life to reveal the core truths that had shaped me.

The memoir didn't achieve significant commercial success, but the responses I received were heartfelt and genuine. I had touched lives and spread awareness amongst a fraction of the society. Readers reached out to me, sharing how my story had inspired them, how it had given them the courage to pursue their own dreams or come to terms with their identity. That was the real success—knowing that I had connected with people on a deeply personal level. I shared my journey, not as a "finished" product, but as a work in progress. I wanted to be seen, to show people that we are part of the world, and that our stories matter.

Amidst all of this, there was another dream that had been simmering quietly—the dream of flying. Ever since I was a child, I had been fascinated by the idea of soaring through the skies, of seeing the world from a different perspective. I began training to become a pilot, studying diligently, and pushing my physical and mental limits to achieve the commercial pilot's license.

Flying was exhilarating. The feeling of lifting off the runway, of breaking free from the earth's grasp, was unlike anything I had ever experienced. There were days of frustration and setbacks, but the goal had taken a back seat and somewhere down the lane, I had forgotten all about dreams like this. I don't know if it was destiny or my hardwork or the blessings from the people in my journey or the wonder of the almighty or the combination of everything, I was able to get the wings pinned on my shirt. I could fly! One childhood desire turning into reality was definitely a strong propelling push for me in the right direction. I would often look down at the roads below from the cockpit, and a part of me would remember the freedom I used to feel on my bike. But life had taken me on a different path now upwards, into the clouds. By the time I achieved my commercial pilot's license, I was aware that I had accomplished this at an age when many pilots had already taken on the responsibilities of a captain. But my path had never been conventional. I took pride in my resilience, in how I had managed to carve out a new life for myself, against the odds.

As I achieved these milestones—writer, author, pageant contestant, pilot—I made it a point to be visible, to stand in the spotlight and represent my community. I gave interviews, conducted seminars, and attended panel discussions to raise awareness about the LGBTQ+ community. I wanted people to see us, not just as a separate group, but as part of the fabric of society, deserving acceptance and equal opportunities.

I was often asked about my journey, about the challenges that I faced, and what kept me going. The answer was always the same: it was the drive to be free, to live authentically. I wanted to create spaces where others like me could feel safe, where our stories could be told without fear or shame, by making it a normal thing for someone like me to be seen amongst the masses. The world was changing, albeit slowly, and I wanted to be a catalyst for that change.

Amid all these achievements, I didn't realize that something was missing. My passion for biking had been put on hold as I chased one dream after another. But the open road was always there, waiting for me to return, quietly reminding me that the freedom I sought was the same freedom I used to feel on my bike. It wasn't gone; it was only hiding, waiting for the right moment to resurface.

The years from 2019 to 2023 were a time of transformation. I became a different person, achieving things I once thought were out of reach. But as I looked back, I realized that my journey was far from over. There were more roads to travel, both literal and metaphorical, and I was ready to find my way back to the passions that had always been with me, even if they had faded into the background. I had become a ghostwriter, a pageant queen, a published author, and a pilot. But somewhere beneath all those achievements was still the girl who loved the roar of an engine, the thrill of acceleration, and the wind against her skin. It was time to rediscover that part of myself, and I knew the open road would be waiting.

The Reel Road

The influence of movies on our lives is undeniable, but for me, biker movies did more than just entertain—they helped shape my identity as a biker and gave me a deeper understanding of the culture, freedom, and spirit associated with riding.

It was through these films that I found a place where the open road was celebrated as a place of self-discovery, rebellion, and personal freedom. From Hollywood to Bollywood, biker films provided me with a glimpse into a world that I felt I belonged to, even before I had the courage to claim it. These movies made me realize that my love for biking wasn't limited by gender norms and that women could ride with just as much passion as men.

The movies I watched didn't just entertain me; they moulded my "biker heart" and became a compass pointing me toward the freedom of the road. The journeys on-screen mirrored the journeys I yearned to undertake, not just across highways and mountains but within my own soul.

One of my earliest memories of biker films was watching *Easy Rider* (1969), an icon for its portrayal of the counterculture of the '60s, freedom, and the desire to break away from society's expectations. The sight of Peter Fonda and Dennis Hopper cruising down long American highways on their choppers stirred something deep inside me. I remember being mesmerized by the visual language of the film—long, open stretches of road, the sun setting over the horizon, and the wind blowing through their hair.

It was a call to freedom, a life unrestricted by the conventions I was always expected to conform to. Watching *Easy Rider* as a young adult, I found myself identifying with the characters' search for meaning and purpose. I wasn't living in America, and I wasn't riding a Harley, but the essence of the journey—the quest for personal freedom and authenticity—resonated deeply with me. The rebellious spirit of the film made me realize that I could seek my own path, even if it didn't align with traditional expectations.

The iconic image of Fonda riding with the American flag emblazoned on his jacket was more than just a symbol of American freedom; it was a representation of an individual's freedom, something that I craved. The open road became a metaphor for the freedom I longed for, both in terms of my gender identity and my desire to live life on my terms.

Another film that left a mark was *The Wild One* (1953), with Marlon Brando's portrayal of Johnny Strabler, the leader of a motorcycle gang. The movie sparked my interest in the culture and history of biking. Brando's character was the embodiment of rebellion and non-conformity. The iconic line, "What are you rebelling against?" followed by his cool, nonchalant answer, "What've you got?" became etched in my memory. It made me realize that biking was not just about the machine; it was about the attitude, the lifestyle, and the courage to break away from the norm.

The film depicted bikers as outsiders, rebels against societal expectations, and in that, I found something I could relate to. At the time, I was struggling to understand my gender identity, feeling like an outsider myself. Watching *The Wild One* helped me see that being different didn't have to be something to hide; it could be a source of strength, a part of my identity to embrace.

Then came *Mad Max* (1979), with its dystopian portrayal of a world where bikers ruled the road in a lawless landscape. The film showed biking as a means of survival, not just an escape, but a way to reclaim control over one's destiny. The roaring engines, the dust clouds rising from the desolate highways, and the raw energy of the bikers painted a picture of resilience and grit.

What resonated with me in *Mad Max* was the idea that bikers could be both the outlaws and the heroes. They were characters shaped by hardship but defined by their determination. It was empowering to see that even in the most broken of worlds, there was still the possibility of freedom, and that riding was a way to assert that freedom. For me, the road symbolized not just a physical journey but an emotional one, an opportunity to break free from the constraints imposed by society.

For the longest time, motorcycling was seen as a male-dominated pursuit, a symbol of rugged masculinity. But movies began to challenge that notion, showing women not just as passive passengers but as riders in their own right. I remember seeing *Thelma & Louise* (1991) and feeling a rush of excitement. Though not primarily a biker film, the movie captured the spirit of rebellion and freedom that comes with being on the open road. The characters, Thelma and Louise, embodied courage and defiance, and their journey was a beautiful mix of liberation and tragedy.

Watching them drive through the vast American landscape made me realize that the road didn't discriminate; it was there for anyone who dared to ride it. The image of Louise on her bike, hair blowing in the wind, was powerful. It gave me the assurance that femininity and the love for bikes could coexist. There was no rulebook that said motorcycles were for men only.

Later, I came across *Torque* (2004), a Hollywood action film with Monica, a fierce female biker who could race and perform stunts with the best of them. Seeing a woman handle a bike with such confidence and aggression shattered the stereotypes I had always seen in mainstream media. It was exhilarating and affirming to see that women could ride with the same ferocity as men, and that biking wasn't about gender—it was about passion and skill. It was then that I began to realize that my own love for biking was not tied to the idea of masculinity; it was something deeper, something pure and authentic that transcended societal labels.

Bollywood, too, had its share of road trip-themed films that made an impact on me. One of the earliest was *Dil Chahta Hai* (2001), where a significant portion of the film revolves around a road trip although in a car from Mumbai to Goa. The film captured the camaraderie, adventure, and sense of freedom that comes with a road trip. Watching the characters bond over their shared love for the open road made me think about my own solo journeys and the friends I made along the way. It wasn't always about reaching a destination; it was about the journey itself, the people you meet, and the experiences you gather.

In *Dhoom* (2004), Bollywood took biking to the next level, with high-speed chases, sleek sports bikes, and the thrill of the chase. The film's portrayal of bikers as adrenaline junkies was electrifying, and the stunts gave me goosebumps. Even though it was an action-packed film, it wasn't just the bikes that fascinated me. It was the freedom that came with riding one—the wind in your face, the heart-pounding speed, and the sense of being invincible. The film made me want to push boundaries, not just on the road but in my life. It inspired me to take risks and challenge my own limits.

While movies provided me with fictional stories of bikers, documentaries gave me a glimpse into real-life biker culture. One such documentary that left a lasting impact was *Why We Ride* (2013), which delved into the stories of different riders, from racers to adventurers, and explored their motivations for riding. The film celebrated the joy and passion of biking, showing that riding was not just a hobby but a way of life, a philosophy.

Watching the documentary, I saw riders of all ages, genders, and backgrounds talking about how biking made them feel alive, how it connected them to the world in a way that nothing else could. There were stories of healing, self-discovery, and personal transformation, and I could relate to so much of what was said. It was a powerful affirmation that my love for biking wasn't just a phase; it was an integral part of who I was.

Another documentary that influenced me was *21 Days Under the Sky* (2016), which followed a group of friends on a cross-country motorcycle trip. The rawness of the film, the challenges they faced, and the bond they shared reminded me of my own travels and the sense of belonging I found on the road. The documentary showed that biking was more than just riding a machine; it was about connection—connection to the road, to oneself, and to those who shared the journey.

Throughout my life, these biker movies and documentaries became more than just entertainment; they were guiding lights that shaped my understanding of freedom, identity, and the biker spirit. The films showed me that the love for biking transcends gender, culture, and background. It doesn't matter if you're a man, a woman, or someone in between; the road is open to all who seek it.

I realized that the road was a place where I could find myself and lose myself at the same time. It was a space where societal expectations faded, where the wind carried away doubts and fears. The characters and stories I encountered in these movies taught me that biking wasn't about fitting into a mold—it was about breaking free from it.

These films helped me embrace the fact that my passion for riding wasn't defined by masculinity or femininity; it was an expression of the soul. The women riders I saw in films and documentaries further affirmed that being a biker wasn't tied to a gender norm—it was about a love for the ride, the connection with the machine, and the freedom that came with it.

There were many nights when I would sit alone in my room, surrounded by the glow of the TV screen, watching biker movies and documentaries, dreaming of the day I could embody that freedom. Each film would ignite a desire to experience what the characters did, to push my limits, to see how far the road could take me. In those moments, I wasn't just a spectator; I was living vicariously through each character's journey.

Watching *Easy Rider* for the first time as a teenager, I felt an inexplicable longing to escape, to ride away from the confines of my own life. The film became a mental escape, where I could imagine a world where I wasn't restricted by societal norms or my own uncertainties.

Years later, when I watched *Torque*, seeing a woman ride a bike with such ferocity made me question why I had ever felt that biking was something tied to masculinity. It was then that I realized I had unconsciously accepted societal labels, but the road itself did not judge.

Similarly, after watching *Why We Ride*, I started seeing my own journeys as more than just trips from one place to another. They were adventures in self-discovery, each ride an opportunity to understand more about who I was and where I wanted to go. The documentaries didn't just show me bikers; they showed me kindred spirits who shared the same love for the road that I did.

The biker movies and documentaries I watched didn't just influence my love for bikes; they shaped my perspective on freedom, rebellion, and self-expression. The lessons I learned from the characters, the roads, and the spirit of riding in these films helped me embrace who I was, without being defined by labels.

Movies like *Easy Rider*, *Ghostrider, The Wild One*, *Mad Max*, *Thelma & Louise*, *Dil Chahta Hai*, and *Dhoom*, along with documentaries like *Why We Ride* and *21 Days Under the Sky*, contributed to moulding my "biker heart." They taught me that the road was for everyone, regardless of gender, and that the thrill of riding wasn't about fitting in but about standing out. As I look back on the influence these films had on my life, I realize that they played a crucial role in my journey of self-acceptance and discovery. The characters may have been fictional, but the emotions they evoked were real, and they resonated with my own experiences as a biker, dreamer, and individual seeking freedom.

The Road Reclaimed

Relocating to Hyderabad felt like opening a new chapter in my life's story—a story that was already full of plot twists, transformations, and bold decisions. Taking on the role of a commercial pilot was both thrilling and challenging, but the city had more to offer than just professional opportunities. Hyderabad's energy seeped into my life in unexpected ways, and with every street I explored, it called to a part of me I hadn't realized I had put on hold.

My work took up most of my time, but there was something about Hyderabad that kept pulling me back to my roots. The city had a distinct pulse, filled with people who were eager to chase dreams, whether professional or personal. I started noticing them all around me—the bikers, their machines rumbling through the streets, their jackets proudly displaying patches from clubs and trips.

One night, scrolling through Instagram, I stumbled upon the page for *Bikerni Hyderabad*, an all-women's biker group. Their feed was a tapestry of freedom, passion, and resilience, with photos of women on bikes, riding through sun-drenched roads, misty mountain paths, and open highways that stretched endlessly ahead. Each image was alive with stories of strength and adventure, and it rekindled a fire within me that had never truly died out.

Every photo, every video, and every post told a story of women who had embraced their love for biking, unafraid to claim a space on the road. There were glimpses of weekend trips, meetups, early morning rides, and late-night adventures. They were young and old, students, mothers, professionals, united by their shared passion for riding. I found myself scrolling through the feed, heart racing, already imagining myself as part of this incredible sisterhood.

The posts from Bikerni Hyderabad did more than just fascinate me—they reminded me that riding had been an essential part of who I was. I couldn't ignore it anymore. I knew that I wanted my bike back, and the thought grew until I picked up my phone, dialled my sister in Delhi, and waited for her to answer.

My sister answered after a few rings, her voice bright with the joy of hearing from me. "Hey there! How's Hyderabad treating you?"
I didn't waste any time. "Guess what? I'm bringing my bike back! I can't ignore it anymore; the bikers here have gotten me all fired up again."
She laughed, the kind of warm, knowing laugh that only a sister could have. "I had a feeling this would happen eventually. It's just been sitting here, gathering dust. Do you know how to get it here?"

We spent the next few minutes going over logistics—me flying in, packing the bike, setting up a courier service. But as practical as the conversation was, beneath it was a thrill that couldn't be contained. I was talking about my bike again, the hum of the engine, the feel of the throttle under my hand, the exhilaration of the open road. My sister seemed to understand this, and her support was clear in her words.

"Don't worry, I'll keep her safe until you get here," she promised, and I felt a warmth that wasn't just about family—it was about feeling seen.

The weekend couldn't come soon enough, and when it did, I boarded my flight to Delhi with a sense of anticipation I hadn't felt in years.

Landing in Delhi felt like coming home in a different way. It wasn't just the familiarity of the city but the thought of reuniting with my bike that made my heart race. My sister picked me up, and the entire ride back, we talked about nothing but the bike. She teased me about my obsession, but I could see she understood how much this meant to me.

When we arrived, I rushed to the garage, and there it was—my bike, a bit dusty, but as powerful and majestic as I remembered. I spent the afternoon cleaning her, checking the engine, and preparing her for the journey ahead. Every turn of the wrench, every wipe of the cloth was like reconnecting with an old friend. It wasn't just a machine; it was a part of my soul, a piece of who I was.

Packing it up was a project in itself. The courier service was shocked to see the plywood box reinforced with pillows along the walls for cushioning, something which I had made when I bought the bike. The entire package weighed nearly 450 kilograms, and watching it all sealed up, ready for transit, filled me with a mix of excitement and impatience. The week ahead would be one of waiting, but I knew that the end of it held the promise of freedom.

Back in Hyderabad, I counted down the days, envisioning myself riding through the city, the wind in my hair (bullshit! How the hell would wind hit my hair, if I were to wear a helmet), the hum of the engine a symphony that I had missed for so long. Finally, the day arrived, and I practically flew down the stairs to greet the truck as it pulled up in front of my building.

The delivery team brought the box down carefully, and there it was—450 kilograms of memories, freedom, and dreams. I wasted no time, opening the box with the excitement of a child unwrapping a present. Piece by piece, my bike emerged, still as beautiful as the day I first rode it. I reconnected the battery terminals, carefully put the fuse back into its compartment, and poured some petrol into the tank from a bottle I had kept ready.

The moment of truth came as I turned the key and pressed the ignition. The engine roared to life, a familiar sound that was music to my ears. It felt like a reunion, like a piece of myself had returned. I sat there for a moment, just listening, before giving the throttle a twist and feeling the bike respond with a growl. She was back, and so was I.

My first stop was the Rynox store. I needed a new jacket, and I had connected with Deekshitha, a fellow biker and member of another biker's club in Hyderabad, who agreed to meet me there. She rode a TVS Ronin and had the same passion for the road as I did. This meeting felt symbolic—a chance to blend the old and new, to start fresh while honoring my past.

I rode to Rynox with an exhilaration that only comes from the first ride after a long time away. The road was open, and I felt like I was flying, the wind a constant companion. At the store, I met Praneeth, the manager and an off-road specialist, who greeted me with a nod, immediately sensing the excitement in my eyes. Praneeth guided me to a line of jackets, but I already knew what I wanted. My old Cramster jacket had been my faithful companion on many journeys, and seeing a Cramster jacket in the store brought back a wave of nostalgia. I chose a blue one, similar in style but new, a representation of the fresh start I was embarking on.

Deekshitha arrived soon after, her son in tow, and we greeted each other like old friends. She was warm and genuine, a woman whose love for biking was palpable. We spent the next hour at the store, browsing, sharing stories, and bonding over our shared passion. Praneeth took photos of us outside, and I posed with my bike, proud and eager to capture this moment.

Praneeth mentioned a weekend night meetup happening at Rynox, a gathering of local bikers. The thought of meeting even more riders was exhilarating, and I spent the next few days preparing, eager to immerse myself in Hyderabad's biker culture. When the night finally came, I dressed in my new jacket, paired it with jeans, and opted for my trusty Quechua ankle boots since I didn't have biker boots yet.

Arriving at Rynox that night was like entering a mini festival for bikers. The parking lot was filled with bikes of different models and make, gleaming under the streetlights. The rumble of engines, the excited chatter, the smell gasoline—it was a sensory overload, and I loved every bit of it.
I was introduced to Shweta, the leader of *Moto Bikers*, a group dedicated to uniting women riders, much like Bikerni. I had been in touch with Shweta for over a week and through her, I had connected with Deekshitha, although I happened to meet Deekshitha before Shweta.

Shweta's presence was confident and inviting, and she introduced me to Lakshmi chechi, a Royal Enfield Meteor 350 rider whose stories of solo trips left me in awe. Harpy on her Hero Impulse, Vijeta - who rode a Bajaj Avenger, and Jacob, another Avenger rider, brought their own tales of rides and camaraderie. Jazz, a professional bike racer, shared stories of her competitions, while Sreen, who rode an RE Interceptor, laughed along, sharing moments of his own adventures. Each person had a story, each ride a memory. The night was filled with laughter, the camaraderie palpable, and I felt as though I had found my tribe.

The meetup had quizzes, with trivia questions about bikes and biking culture. I surprised myself by winning a T-shirt—a small prize, but one that meant a lot. By the end of the night, we decided to head to Via Moka, a café owned by Harjeet ji, an entrepreneur and rider himself. The ambiance was warm and filled with a sense of belonging. The place had a nice open sitting with minimal décor, giving the café a nostalgic, rustic feel. As we gathered at a large table, the conversations flowed, each of us sharing stories of our rides, our struggles, and the roads that had led us to this moment.

Deekshitha shared her experience of balancing her roles as a mother and a biker, while Shweta talked about her dream of organizing an all-women cross-country ride, something she hoped would inspire more women to join the community. Harpy spoke of her initial fear of riding alone and how she was coping up with learning the nuances of dirt biking, and Lakshmi chechi talked about the reactions she received as a female rider on her Royal Enfield Meteor—some were supportive, while others questioned her choices, but she rode on with pride and determination, which also gave her a wider purpose in life.

As the night wore on, I realized that each of us had a story that made us unique, yet our love for the road had woven our paths together. It was past 2:30 in the morning when we finally parted ways, the streets of Hyderabad quiet and serene. I rode back home, the night air cool against my face, and felt a profound sense of gratitude. This city, these people, and my return to the biking world had given me a new sense of purpose.

As I parked my bike and looked back at the road I had just travelled, I knew this was only the beginning. There would be many more rides, countless stories, and a lifetime of memories waiting to be made. The road ahead was open, inviting, and filled with possibilities. And this time, I was ready to embrace every mile.

Hyderabad's Road To Heartfelt Connections

Moving to Hyderabad introduced me to a side of the city far beyond its historic Charminar, bustling IT hubs, or famous biryani. Hyderabad held a vibrant biking community, filled with people from diverse backgrounds, each bringing their own energy to the city's roads. The names of groups like *Hyderabad United Bikers (HUB)*, *Biker Knights*, *ATH*, *Bikerni Hyderabad*, *Kirak Riderz*, *HYDE*, and *Telangana Women Moto Bikers* were as unique as the riders themselves. Each group represented a different shade of the city's dynamic biker soul.

One of the first communities that welcomed me was *Moto Bikers* later rechristened as *Telangana Women Moto Bikers*; an all-women group led by Shweta. Shweta's leadership was magnetic—she was a blend of strength and calm, inspiring everyone around her. Through Moto Bikers, I met some of the most incredible women, each with their own story of courage and passion.

There was Javeleen, a powerhouse rider whose inner strength shone on every ride. Shreya brought infectious enthusiasm, while Utkarsha brought the energy of Delhi around us! Shanthi and Madhu brought maturity, patience and the strength to solve dilemmas! Veronica and Deekshitha were seasoned riders either going solo or had previous experience with groups in different cities. Vijeta's presence added tranquility, reminding us all to savor each moment on the road.

And then there was Sheba, a confident, seasoned rider who worked at *Hero MotoCorp*. Sheba's influence extended beyond *Moto Bikers*; she was the founder of *Valkyrie*, Hyderabad's third all-women biking club, and was contributing to empowering women riders in the city, like the other two groups. Her drive, her elegance on the bike, and her unwavering confidence made her a role model for many of us. Sheba showed us that biking was a journey without limitations, where women could lead, inspire, and create new paths for future riders.

Beyond *Moto Bikers*, I discovered a tapestry of other groups that added richness to Hyderabad's biking culture. The *Biker Knights* were like a family—welcoming, supportive, and always ready to lend a hand to anyone in need. *Freedom Riding Group*, true to their name, thrived on exploration. Their rides were about more than just destinations—they were about challenging oneself and finding meaning in the journey. The *Kirak Riders* and *ATH*, however, brought a daring energy to the mix, organizing night rides, off roading and embracing speed with a rebellious spirit that turned every ride into an exhilarating experience. *HYDE* was known for their meticulous rides, with every event carefully coordinated and executed. Riding with HYDE felt like a performance, with each member bringing their own style and precision.

Another deeply inspiring group was *Bikerni Hyderabad*, the all-women's club that represented strength and independence. Meeting Anisah Fatima Latheef, who leads *Bikerni Hyderabad*, brought to light the courage it took for women to carve their space in a world often dominated by men. "The road is where I feel free," Ayesha shared one evening over coffee, her eyes filled with determination. For her, and many like her, biking wasn't just a pastime—it was liberation. She juggles life owning and managing a gym with her passion for reading books, writing blogs and organising bike rides to explore.

Sunday mornings hold a special place in Hyderabad's biker community with the tradition of breakfast rides. Riders would gather in the early hours, bikes gleaming under the dawn sky, and set off to cozy dhabas and Udipi cafés for a meal together or just to ride and explore new places. It was in these early hours, over plates of dosas and cups of hot chai, that I truly got to know the people who made Hyderabad's biking community feel like home.

One memorable breakfast ride brought me next to someone whom we can call Dr. X, a doctor by profession. "On the road, I'm just another rider," he said, sipping his chai. "It's where I leave the stress behind." His words resonated deeply, reminding me that biking was a sanctuary, a place where titles didn't matter, and everyone was united by a shared love for the open road.

Sheba's journey went beyond her personal love for bikes. As a professional at *Hero MotoCorp*, she led with both skill and grace, but her commitment to empowering women was equally remarkable. Through *Valkyrie*, she created a space for women riders to connect, learn, and grow. Watching Sheba balance her career with her role as the founder of *Valkyrie* was inspiring—a reminder that biking was more than just a passion; it was a platform for change.

Hyderabad's bikers rode not only for adventure but for meaningful causes. The *Distinguished Gentleman's Ride (DGR)* brought together hundreds of riders, dressed in their finest suits, to raise awareness for men's health. The *Flag Ride for Independence Day* was a patriotic celebration, where bikers carried the tricolor with pride, united in a display of national pride and solidarity. Each event carried a purpose, reminding me that biking could be a force for good. Joining the *Say No to Drugs Ride* was an experience that went beyond the thrill of the road; it was about spreading a message of positivity and health. These rides showed me that Hyderabad's biker community was built on values—freedom, unity, and responsibility.

In Hyderabad, I discovered not only a love for biking but a community that felt like family. Each ride, each conversation, and each friendship was a reminder of why I fell in love with biking in the first place. From Shweta's unwavering leadership in *Moto Bikers* to Sheba's vision with *Valkyrie*, from the thrill of *ATH* to the warmth of *HYDE*, every moment added a new chapter to my journey. Hyderabad's biking culture was more than a community; it was a way of life. It was a reminder that the road was for everyone—regardless of gender, background, or profession. And as I parked my bike at the end of another ride, I knew that this city, these people, and this road would always be a part of me.

Redefining Sisterhood & Brotherhood

Transitioning to live as a woman was a journey filled with both joy and challenges, but one of the hurdles that persisted was my relationship with men. Over the years, I had largely stayed away from forming close connections with them, finding comfort and understanding mainly among women. With men, I carried an underlying fear, a hesitance that came from a mix of past experiences and my own insecurities.

In the beginning, I expected a similar pattern within Hyderabad's biker community. I assumed that my role would revolve around the women I'd bonded with, like Shweta, Vijeta and Sheba. I had limited expectations from male riders, fearing their judgment, and often kept to myself around them, avoiding eye contact and interaction. I feared they might laugh behind my back or make dismissive comments about my identity. But slowly, the riders I met in Hyderabad—Praneeth, Jacob, Hafiz, Sunny, John, and Shawn, among others—began to show me that there was space for acceptance, understanding, and genuine friendship.

Jacob and Sunny were two of the first male riders who approached me with warmth and respect. They were regulars in the biker meetups and had an easy-going confidence about them, one that didn't carry a hint of prejudice. Jacob, a big-hearted guy with an infectious laugh, was well-known for his kindness and willingness to help everyone. Sunny, with his calm and measured approach, was Jacob's perfect counterpart.

During one ride, I remember a guy casually riding alongside me, matching my pace. I could feel his curiosity, not in a probing way but in a genuinely friendly one. Eventually, he struck up a conversation about the practicality of owning a Harley Davidson. "That's a rare colour and a good choice of bike," he said when we stopped a little ahead. His words felt like a validation of my efforts, a signal that he saw me first as a biker, a person, rather than a transwoman.

Sunny, on the other hand, was more reserved but incredibly respectful. He would share his riding tips, speak about routes, and exchange biker knowledge without ever hinting at the prejudices I'd once feared. One day after a ride, as we all relaxed at a café, he leaned over and said, "You know, your dedication to riding is inspiring. It's clear you love the road." His words had a quiet sincerity that began to erode my defences.

Over time, more men in the group began to feel like genuine friends, but it was John Cheta and Shawn who left an indelible impact. John Cheta, older than most riders, was like an elder brother to all of us. He had this calm authority about him, a wisdom and humour, that made everyone gravitate towards him. I had never thought I could connect with someone like him, but his warmth made it impossible not to.

One evening after a ride, a small group of us gathered at a roadside stall, enjoying chai and discussing plans for upcoming rides. As we talked about favorite destinations and must-see places, I mentioned the thrill of the mountain routes I had once taken to Leh. With genuine curiosity, one of the guys asked me, "How did you manage those long rides? Must've been tough." His question was more than casual; it was laced with respect and admiration. Here was someone who saw beyond gender and identity, who saw the biker in me.

Shawn, in his own way, was equally encouraging. Younger than me but brimming with enthusiasm, Shawn had a natural charm and easy humor that made every interaction enjoyable. We started talking more during group dinners, where I found myself laughing, joining in on their stories, and slowly letting go of my initial reluctance. Shawn's approach was simple—he never hesitated to include me, never hesitated to invite me into conversations or events, making me feel valued in a way I hadn't felt in a long time.

One evening, Shawn invited me to dinner at *Fisherman's Wharf*, a popular spot known for its Goan cuisine and relaxed ambiance. It was my first one-on-one outing with a man since I'd started my transition, and I couldn't help but feel both excited and nervous. Fisherman's Wharf was bustling with energy that night, the sound of clinking glasses and laughter creating a lively backdrop.

As we sat down and ordered, Shawn made it a point to talk about biking, avoiding the usual small talk that often felt forced. Instead, he shared his own challenges on the road, asking about mine with genuine interest. At one point, he laughed, saying, "The road doesn't care about who you are—only that you respect it. That's what I see in you. You respect the ride."

Shawn's words were simple, but they were also transformative. Here was a man who didn't feel the need to bring up my identity, to question, or to judge. We were just two people sharing a meal, two bikers talking about the road. It was an experience that began to reshape my understanding of friendship with men.

Hyderabad's biker community didn't just limit itself to rides; it was a close-knit group that celebrated birthdays, holidays, and every other reason to gather. Through these outings, I began to interact with more men, each one chipping away at the walls I had built over time.

At one party, I remember sitting with a small group, listening to another guy tell a story about a breakdown he had in the middle of nowhere. His vivid description had us all laughing, and at some point, he turned to me and asked, "Have you ever had one of those nightmare breakdowns? You know, the kind that makes you wonder if you'll ever get back on the road?"

Without hesitation, I shared my own experience of a breakdown near Chandigarh, where I'd had to stay overnight, all because I'd forgotten to check the engine oil. Instead of laughing at my misfortune, they laughed with me, teasing me like they would any other friend. It was in those small moments that I realized these men saw me as an equal, as a fellow biker who shared in their love for the road.

Riding with Hyderabad's biker community gave me a sense of belonging I hadn't anticipated. The respect I received wasn't conditional or half-hearted; it was genuine and extended freely. They appreciated my discipline, my commitment to safety, and my enthusiasm for each ride. It was an unspoken bond, one that didn't need validation or explanation.

During one group ride, as we sped through Hyderabad's outskirts, the sun setting in the background, I felt a sense of freedom and acceptance that went beyond words. Riding beside Jacob and Sunny, I realized I was no longer "different" in their eyes. I was just another rider, part of the team, united by our shared love for biking.

Through Hyderabad's biker clubs, my relationship with men transformed in ways I hadn't imagined possible. Each ride, each gathering, and each conversation built a new foundation of trust, respect, and camaraderie. Jacob, Sunny, John, Shawn, and the other male riders I grew close to showed me that men could be allies, friends, and genuine sources of support.

It wasn't just about the rides or the parties; it was about the comfort they offered, the laughter we shared, and the understanding that grew naturally between us. These men didn't see me as a transwoman but as a biker, a friend, a person with whom they shared a common passion. For them, my gender identity was a mere detail, something secondary to the spirit of riding.

As I reflect on my time with Hyderabad's biker community, I realize that they redefined brotherhood for me. They showed me that friendship could be inclusive, that men could be understanding, and that there was space for acceptance in places I hadn't expected. The bonds I formed were not only strong but transformative, shaping my understanding of friendship and respect.

This journey on Hyderabad's roads was more than a journey of miles; it was a journey of healing, acceptance, and growth. I was no longer just a biker; I was part of a community, a family that embraced me, supported me, and showed me that true friendship transcends labels.

Distinguished Gentleman's Ride

The *Distinguished Gentleman's Ride* (DGR) began as a small initiative in 2012, envisioned by Mark Hawwa in Sydney, Australia. This event was inspired by a scene from the TV series *Mad Men* where a character rides a classic motorcycle in a suit, challenging the characteristic image associated with bikers. Hawwa's dream was to form an event at a global scale where bikers could dapper up and also raise awareness and funds for men's mental health and prostate cancer. The first DGR was held with a few hundred bikers in suits, but it quickly gained popularity, becoming an annual event that would unite bikers worldwide. It's a day where thousands of riders don tailored suits, meet up on their bikes, hit the road, and celebrate not just their passion for motorcycles but also their commitment to making a difference in the lives of people.

It was a casual scroll through my *Moto Bikers* group chat that introduced me to DGR. The post about an upcoming DGR in Hyderabad immediately caught my eye. My heart raced, intrigued by the thought of riding for such a meaningful cause. But just as quickly as excitement set in, hesitation followed. Riding in a full suit under Hyderabad's unrelenting sun? It felt both thrilling and impractical.

Shweta and Vijeta were quick to encourage me, sending me enthusiastic messages, hyping up the event's significance, and insisting that I join. Despite my hesitation, they didn't take "no" for an answer, and their insistence struck a chord. Finally, after some gentle nudging, I gave in and registered, feeling both anxious and eager.

With my registration complete, the next challenge was the outfit. As I opened my wardrobe, a bronze satin shirt gleamed in the light. I paired it with beige pants, but I knew it needed something more to complete the "distinguished" look. Determined to find the right piece, I headed to the mall to search for a waistcoat or half-jacket.
Navigating through the bustling aisles at *Pantaloons*, I finally spotted the perfect waistcoat—a muted shade that matched my pants while adding just the right amount of formality. I left the store feeling confident, picturing how I'd look riding in this outfit, embracing both the elegance and the purpose of the day.

The next morning, I was up early, slipping into the outfit with a sense of excitement and pride. The bronze shirt felt cool against my skin, the waistcoat adding a sense of sophistication. As I laced up my brown boots, a calm excitement settled over me. This was going to be more than just a ride; it was a journey with meaning.

By 6 a.m., the streets were quiet, the dawn breeze refreshing. Riding toward *Sanjeevaiah Park*, I felt anticipation building with each turn, knowing I was joining something bigger than myself.

As I arrived, *Sanjeevaiah Park* was already filled with an incredible array of motorcycles and bikers, all dressed to the nines in elegant suits and classic outfits. There were vintage Royal Enfields, sleek Triumphs, and custom Harley-Davidsons, each bike unique, and each rider proud.

Shweta, Vijeta, and other familiar faces from *Moto Bikers* greeted me with compliments and smiles. “Looking sharp!” Deekshitha exclaimed, giving me an approving nod. I could sense the same excitement in everyone’s faces, the shared understanding that we were part of something meaningful or maybe it was just the excitement of meeting one another for a ride on a weekend!

Jacob and Sunny waved me over with enthusiastic grins, and before I knew it, we were laughing and swapping stories. “Look at us,” Jacob said, gesturing to the crowd. “This has to be the best-dressed gang Hyderabad has ever seen!” His comment lightened the atmosphere, and soon, everyone was joking and laughing as we admired each other’s attire.

I met Vaani, a fellow rider I hadn't known before. Her enthusiasm was contagious as we bonded over our mutual love for riding and the thrill of being part of the DGR. We shared stories of past rides, and I felt a deep sense of camaraderie that only grew stronger as the morning unfolded.

The organizers gathered us for a briefing, and the excitement in the air was palpable. Engines revved as the flag-off was announced, and our group set off in two columns, riding in perfect formation. The early morning sun cast a golden glow on the streets, and I could feel the eyes of passersby watching us with a mixture of awe and curiosity.
As we rode through Hyderabad, people paused, fascinated by the sight of bikers in suits. It felt empowering to be part of this display of elegance and purpose, knowing we were riding for a cause that extended beyond the road.

The ride had its challenges, with a few riders occasionally breaking formation, but the marshals kept the group organized, guiding everyone back into the columns. Most of us followed the guidelines, moving in sync as we navigated Hyderabad's streets. Riding through the city felt exhilarating, each turn a reminder of the unity and purpose that brought us together.

The resort greeted us with its tranquil setting, a beautiful contrast to the lively energy of the ride. We parked, and the cameras began flashing as riders took turns posing with their bikes, capturing the spirit of the day. The breakfast spread was a welcome sight, and we gathered around to enjoy the food, exchanging stories and laughter.

Sitting with Vaani, we shared tales of our favorite rides, our dreams of future journeys, and our shared excitement for the event. The sense of community was profound, each interaction deepening the bonds we had formed on the road.

When the awards were announced, I was stunned to hear my name called for the *Best Dressed Biker*. The applause and cheers from my friends were overwhelming as I stepped forward to accept the award. Holding the prize, I felt a wave of pride and gratitude. This wasn't just an award; it was a recognition of my journey, my identity, and the support of a community that embraced me wholeheartedly.

Riding back home, I felt a deep sense of fulfilment. The Distinguished Gentleman's Ride had been more than a ride; it was a celebration of purpose, community, and self-expression. The bonds I formed, the conversations I had, and the cause we supported all resonated deeply within me. It was a reminder that the road was not just a place for individual journeys but a space for unity and impact.

As I parked my bike, I knew that this ride would remain etched in my memory—a testament to the power of community, purpose, and the joy of being part of something greater than oneself.

Dancing With Chaos – Hyderabad's Traffic

The first day I took to the streets of Hyderabad, it felt like stepping into an arena where rules dissolved in the morning heat, leaving only instinct to guide me. The roads were alive, pulsating with energy, but unlike the heartbeat of a city, it was erratic—a thundering pulse without rhythm. Every lane was a battleground where cars, bikes, and pedestrians vied for the smallest scraps of space, each trying to claim a piece of the road.

Riding here was like diving headfirst into a river full of uncharted currents. Hyderabad's roads didn't flow; they churned. Bikers darted through the smallest gaps, autos squeezed between lanes with an unhurried boldness, and buses commanded their path as if each driver were the king of their own realm. The loud, staccato of honking was relentless—a jarring symphony of brakes, screeches, and shouts that seemed to rise and fall like a city-wide chant.

The moment I hit the throttle, I knew this wasn't just about riding; this was about learning to anticipate the unpredictable, to make split-second choices in a landscape of moving parts that barely adhered to the rules I'd taken for granted in other cities. It was both thrilling and unnerving, a test of nerves and patience as every vehicle cut across lanes as if on a dare, leaving me both fascinated and slightly terrified.

Each area in Hyderabad has its own chaotic personality, its own specific blend of urgency and disregard for order. Gachibowli and parts of Secunderabad felt like fleeting mirages of structure—places where lanes seemed to mean something, where right-of-way held value. The IT hub of Gachibowli was like a whisper of restraint, with rows of corporate parks inspiring a semblance of order. Here, drivers seemed to pause, a rare hesitation in their daily dance, as if the unspoken rules tightened their grip around these gleaming buildings.

Yet, leaving these pockets of calm was like descending into a different world, especially when navigating through the bustling streets near Mehdipatnam. The lanes vanished in all but name; boundaries became mere suggestions. In Mehdipatnam, it was survival of the boldest, a place where each car, bike, and auto tried to muscle ahead, asserting dominance with a nonchalant swagger. The very concept of traffic lights seemed optional here, ignored with a confidence that bordered on defiance. Honking wasn't just a way of signalling—it was a language, a territorial claim. Each sound had its own meaning, its own command in this orchestra of metal and will.

It was here, amid this unpredictable chaos, that I began to see driving as less of a right and more of a daily trial. Each road had its own dangers, like a maze that shifted as you walked through it, where the roads bent and blurred, and my senses sharpened to anticipate the unexpected.

Over time, the chaos taught me to read Hyderabad's streets with a fresh pair of eyes. Surviving here wasn't about driving; it was about becoming attuned to the language of the road, the subtle cues, and the signals hidden in every driver's movement. I learned to watch for the slightest lean in a driver's posture, the near imperceptible tilt of a wheel, the sudden halt of an auto. In a place where indicators seemed decorative, I had to read the body language of the cars and bikes around me, predicting their next move with an almost sixth sense. Riders and drivers of Hyderabad could actually beat an AI model in predictive analysis!

Patience became my greatest ally. Every time a car lurched ahead, every time an auto cut across my path, I forced myself to take a breath, to slow down. This city demanded a dance of flexibility, the ability to sway to the rhythm of unpredictability without losing my balance. Rather than trying to master the roads, I let them teach me to be agile, patient, and, above all, cautious. Delhi had once felt chaotic, but time had tempered its pulse. The city had embraced road discipline, a gradual shift that was palpable. The highways once teeming with aggressive drivers had softened, the horns replaced by an occasional honk rather than a constant blare. When I first saw Delhi embracing helmet mandates, lane discipline, and signalling, I felt a pang of pride mixed with disbelief. The city was evolving, and I could see that Delhi's drivers were learning to respect the structure, the unspoken flow that made travel a bit more bearable.

Yet, in Hyderabad, these changes seemed distant. The city seemed to hold tight to its characteristic style—part defiance, part fluidity. Riding here, I missed the growing structure of Delhi, the way lanes had begun to mean something, the way a traffic signal held sway. Hyderabad was still a place where freedom was taken to its extreme, a place where roads felt like battlegrounds.

In contrast, the Secunderabad area offered something close to a reprieve. Here, there was an inkling of respect for the road, a sense that drivers actually observed traffic signals. But going to Secunderabad meant that I was supposed to cross Mehdipatnam, which I couldn't! Navigating these hotspots required a map not just of routes but of strategies. In Mehdipatnam, I learned to ride with a defensive posture, to expect the unexpected. In Secunderabad and Gachibowli, I could relax just a bit, allowing myself to ride without the constant vigilance that other areas demanded.

This mental map of safe zones and chaotic pockets became my compass, my guide to surviving Hyderabad's roads. Amid the turbulence of Hyderabad's streets, biker groups like *Bikerni Hyderabad, TWMB, Kirak Riders* and others emerged as lighthouses, beacons of order, structure, and safety. These groups weren't just a gathering of riders—they were communities committed to a shared purpose, upholding the values of discipline and respect on the road. Riding with them was a reminder that there was still hope for Hyderabad's traffic, a vision of what the roads could look like if more riders and drivers followed their lead.

During rides, the marshals would ride at the front, setting the pace, and guiding the entire column in orderly formation. Helmets were a must, speed limits adhered to, and lane discipline was followed with a reverence that felt almost ceremonial. Riding with these groups was a balm, a respite from the usual chaos, and a way to reconnect with the joy of biking, free from the worries of erratic drivers and unpredictable turns.

The biker clubs organized safety awareness campaigns, helmet drives, and road etiquette workshops. And though their influence felt limited on the grand scale, it was reassuring to see these clubs quietly setting a standard, spreading a message that responsibility on the road wasn't just possible but necessary.

The biker groups took it upon themselves to bring road safety to the public's attention, organizing drives to speak openly about the importance of lane discipline and signalling. The marshals played a key role during these drives, taking up positions to help manage traffic flow, enforce speed limits, and ensure the entire group rode in unison. Riding with a marshal was like having a guardian on the road, someone who could guide and protect.

During one awareness drive, I remember watching as young riders on the sidelines watched us pass, captivated by the sight of bikers in full gear, riding with a sense of purpose. The looks on their faces held a glimmer of admiration, and in those moments, I felt the potential impact these groups could make.

However, changing a city's mindset was a task too massive for any single group. I knew that while the clubs made strides in raising awareness, Hyderabad's traffic culture held fast to its roots. Even with helmet mandates and campaigns, the general attitude toward road safety remained one of indifference, a habit that would take years to reshape.

Hyderabad's roads proved to be more than just chaotic—they were a real and present danger. Every intersection felt like a potential trap, every turn held the possibility of a collision. Here, accidents weren't just possibilities; they were the inevitable consequences of a system that ran on disregard. As much as I loved the city's vibrancy, the roads painted a grim picture of the risks that came with unchecked freedom.

Change wasn't just necessary—it was urgent. Hyderabad's roads carried a beauty and a danger that needed tempering, a balance of freedom and discipline. While the biker clubs represented a glimmer of hope, it was clear that the city had a long way to go. I hoped that, over time, the example set by groups like *Moto Bikers* would ripple out, inspiring more riders to embrace safety and respect.

A Birthday To Remember

The story begins with Shweta, the mastermind behind my first birthday celebration as my true self. She meticulously planned every detail, orchestrating the whole event behind the scenes. Unknown to me, she temporarily removed me from the *Moto Bikers* group the day before my birthday to coordinate the plans. It was a risk but also a testament to her dedication. Shweta contacted each of the women individually, gathering their ideas, and rallying them around the idea of creating a birthday I'd never forget.

The details were set—the venue, the timing, and even the secrecy of it all. *Garage Moto Café*, a favourite spot in Jubilee Hills, was chosen for its laid-back, biker-friendly vibe. As she shared her vision, each friend offered her unique touch to make the celebration unforgettable. The entire plan was set, and I was blissfully unaware of the surprise awaiting me.

On the evening of my birthday, a message from Shweta came through. It was simple yet intriguing: *"Come to Garage Moto Café at 6 p.m. We've got a little something planned for you!"*

I was curious but didn't expect anything extravagant. I'd never celebrated my birthday in a grand way since my transition, and even before, I didn't always mark the day. But the thought of seeing my friends and sharing the day in a relaxed setting was enough to make me look forward to it. Deciding to dress for the occasion, I chose my gift to myself—a beautiful saree from *SuTa*, in black colour with a string of colours that felt celebratory yet elegant. The thought of wearing a saree to a biker café was unconventional, but it felt fitting for such a personal occasion. I put on my favourite earrings, added a touch of lipstick, and looked in the mirror with a mix of excitement and nerves.

As I pulled up to *Garage Moto Café*, I noticed the casual, biker-centric vibe of the place—walls adorned with vintage motorcycle posters, a lineup of gleaming bikes parked outside, and the familiar smell of leather and coffee hanging in the air. Dressed in a saree, I stood out a bit, but it was my birthday, and I felt beautiful, confident, and unapologetically myself.

Inside, I spotted Simi first, already waiting with a big smile. "Happy Birthday!" she exclaimed, pulling me into a warm hug. Just then, I noticed a few more familiar faces trickling in—Madhu, Vijeta, Barbie, Utkarsha, Deekshitha, Harpy, and Shreya. Each greeted me with bright smiles and heartfelt hugs, filling me with gratitude for the thoughtful gestures of each friend.

Seeing my friends gathered in one place, all here to celebrate with me, was deeply moving. As more friends joined, I felt the warmth of each embrace, each "Happy Birthday," like a wave of love. The café was buzzing with energy, yet our corner was especially lively as everyone laughed, shared stories, and exchanged memories. We settled into our seats, and conversations flowed freely as each friend shared memories, laughter, and playful teasing.

The energy was infectious. Harpy recounted a funny moment from one of our group rides, while Utkarsha made a light-hearted joke about my saree. "Only you could pull off a saree at a biker café!" she laughed. I couldn't help but chuckle with her; it was such a unique blend of who I was—a biker, a friend, and a woman proud of her identity.

As everyone gathered, I spotted Shweta bringing out a cake—beautifully decorated and personalized with a simple "Happy Birthday Naina" written in delicate script. My heart swelled with gratitude; this wasn't just any cake. It was a symbol of love, friendship, and acceptance. This was my first birthday cake since I transitioned. This was the first time Naina was written on a cake for me!

The group erupted into a chorus of "Happy Birthday," each voice bringing a sense of joy and sincerity. Standing there, surrounded by friends, I felt a mix of emotions. This was my first birthday celebrated openly as my true self, with people who saw me for who I was and accepted me wholeheartedly. I made a wish, a small, silent one, as I blew out the candles, feeling the warmth of their cheers fill the room.

After the cake, we raised our glasses for a toast. Each of us held a mocktail, colourful and garnished with fresh fruit, as we clinked glasses. Shweta spoke up first, sharing a heartfelt message that left me emotional. "Here's to you, and to the courage it takes to be true to yourself," she said, her voice filled with warmth. Her words resonated deeply, capturing everything I had hoped this day would be.

Each friend chimed in, offering toasts that were as unique as they were, filled with laughter, admiration, and warmth. It was a moment of pure joy, feeling seen, valued, and understood. We sipped our drinks and delved into lively conversations—about bikes, life, and dreams.

The laughter from another table caught my attention, and I noticed a group of guys celebrating nearby. Naveen, another biker, was also having his birthday celebration. As our eyes met, he smiled and raised his glass in acknowledgment. I recognized a few of the men from our biking community, and soon, some of them joined our table for a quick chat. Naveen was charming and lively, and as he shared his birthday with our group, I felt a sense of camaraderie that only the biking community could create. We exchanged stories about our rides, shared memorable moments from past trips, and bonded over our shared love for the open road.
The two birthday celebrations seemed to merge, turning the café into a festive scene filled with laughter, shared stories, and new connections.

As the night went on, I couldn't help but reflect on the significance of this celebration. Growing up, birthdays had always been simple affairs—perhaps a small cake at home, a few friends, but always with a sense of holding back. Celebrating as my authentic self, surrounded by friends who saw me completely, was a deeply moving experience. It felt like reclaiming a part of myself that had been hidden, a chance to truly embrace and celebrate who I was.

I thought back to birthdays in school and college, the last one I had celebrated as a boy, and how different this day felt. This birthday was a statement, a celebration not just of the passing of time but of the journey, the choices, and the courage that had brought me here.

As the party wound down, and the last hugs were shared, I stepped outside the café, letting the gentle night air wash over me. The hum of city life had settled into a calm, the streetlights casting long shadows along the road, as if the world had slowed down, allowing me to savour this moment of solitude. I took a deep breath, closing my eyes for a second, absorbing the laughter, the love, and the joy that had filled the evening.

Standing there, I felt an overwhelming sense of gratitude. This birthday, in its simplicity and warmth, had given me something I had been searching for—acceptance, love, and a sense of belonging that I hadn't fully realized I needed. I thought back to past birthdays, where celebration had always felt slightly incomplete, the true self I was yet to embrace lurking somewhere in the background, yearning to be acknowledged. But today was different. Today, I was embraced as myself, with friends who celebrated the real me, who had seen me for who I was and embraced that journey.

I started back for home in my car. The city lights blurred slightly as I thought of Shweta and her careful planning, the love and dedication behind each small detail. The sparkle in Vijeta's eyes as she raised a toast in my honour, Simi's infectious laughter, the way each friend had shown up, each gesture filled with warmth and sincerity. The beautiful SuTa saree that I had so carefully chosen felt like a badge of honour, marking not just a special day, but a testament to all the steps, big and small, that had brought me here. The saree, the friends, the laughter—they were symbols of a life I had worked hard to build.

As I continued to drive through the quiet streets, scenes from the evening replayed in my mind like snapshots—a kaleidoscope of laughter, hugs, shared stories, and a growing sense of togetherness that had become my foundation. I could still hear Shweta's toast echoing in my head, her words laced with admiration and encouragement. Each friend's face, the precious time they took out for me, each word shared, lingered, filling me with a reassurance I hadn't known I needed.

For the first time in a long time, I felt a sense of forward momentum. This birthday had been a reminder that my journey wasn't one I had to walk alone; there were people who would stand by me, celebrate with me, and even push me to go further than I might go alone. I looked ahead, seeing possibilities open before me—not just in friendships, but in how I could continue to embrace life as my true self, courageously and without reservation. There was something magical about feeling seen, knowing that the life I was building had a place for me to be loved and respected. The drive back was filled with moments of quiet introspection. For so long, birthdays had been days I either shied away from or marked quietly, hesitant to make too much of a fuss. But now, with the support of these friends, my *Moto Bikers* family, the future looked less daunting. I imagined more birthdays like this, more rides, more memories, and the chance to grow even further into who I was meant to be. In the quiet hum of the drive with soft music playing on the stereo, I realized that this birthday was more than just a celebration of another year. It was a celebration of resilience, of perseverance, and of the courage to live fully and unapologetically. I felt the weight of their kindness, the quiet strength of their support wrapping around me, giving me the confidence to look forward with optimism and purpose. The road stretched ahead of me, inviting, open, and full of promise, and I knew that wherever it led, I was ready.

Magic of Gachibowli At Night

The city transformed as night fell, a vibrant landscape of lights and shadows weaving together under the star-speckled sky. The Gachibowli area, Hyderabad's bustling IT district by day, seemed to shed its formal attire as the sun dipped below the horizon. It took on a personality of its own, one filled with energy and mystery, each corner and street pulsing with a new life. The buildings towered above, their sleek silhouettes adorned with shimmering lights, casting long shadows across the streets below. It felt like stepping into a different world, one where anything was possible and where the road, for a few fleeting hours, belonged entirely to me.

With the engine humming steadily beneath me, I felt the connection between myself and my bike, as if we were sharing a quiet understanding. Every gear shift and throttle were a conversation in unspoken words, a mutual agreement to explore the city together, to push beyond the boundaries I'd known and experience Hyderabad as I had never experienced it before. This ride wasn't just a journey through a city—it was an exploration of identity, a moment to fully embrace the freedom I'd found in both my life and on the road.

As I took off down the road, the world around me blurred, the city unfolding before me in streaks of light and movement. Gachibowli at night was a masterpiece in neon and chrome, each turn a brushstroke that added depth to the painting, each streetlight casting new highlights on the roads that twisted and curved ahead. Riding through these streets felt like floating on a river of light, the gentle curve of the road guiding me forward, inviting me to let go of any hesitation and embrace the thrill.

The air was cool against my skin, a gentle reminder of the night's embrace as I leaned into each turn, the rush of wind carrying the city's stories, murmurs, and laughter. It was as if Hyderabad itself was alive, the streets breathing in unison with me, sharing in my excitement, mirroring the pounding of my heart. The night seemed to stretch, becoming a vast expanse of possibility, where every corner I rounded and every stretch of road became an opportunity to delve deeper into this journey of self-discovery.

The buildings in Gachibowli stood like watchful guardians, towering in silent approval, their windows gleaming like a constellation of stars. They seemed to lean in, observing, acknowledging, and perhaps even cheering me on. These structures, both familiar and intimidating, no longer felt daunting. Instead, they felt like old friends, part of a backdrop that was both protective and inviting.

They were a reminder that the journey wasn't just about the destination but the path itself, each moment a brushstroke painting the city with memories, experiences, and dreams.

The roads were not empty, but there was a calmness that came with the night, a sense of order amid the usual chaos of Hyderabad's traffic. Cars passed by, but their pace seemed relaxed, unhurried, as if the city itself had slowed down to appreciate the tranquillity of the night. I fell into a rhythm, one that felt almost musical, as the soft rumble of my engine blended with the distant sounds of other vehicles, the occasional honk, and the gentle hum of voices drifting from open windows.

Every ride through Gachibowli became a dance with the city, a moment to synchronize with its heartbeat. The road curved gently beneath me, guiding me through a landscape that felt both new and familiar. There was a beauty in the contrast—the bustling life during the day, replaced by the quiet serenity of night, each bringing out a different side of Hyderabad. It was a reminder that, just like me, the city had multiple faces, each one as valid and beautiful as the other.

There was something profoundly liberating about riding at night, the knowledge that the road stretched out ahead of me, open and unending. It was a freedom I had grown to cherish, a reminder that the journey was mine to define. The cityscape, with its towering buildings and glittering lights, became a testament to dreams, both fulfilled and yet to be realized. The open road was an invitation to explore those dreams, to chase them with the same intensity and passion that I had brought to this new chapter of my life.

Each stretch of road felt like a canvas, a blank slate on which I could paint my journey, my hopes, my identity. I was no longer just a rider navigating through traffic; I was a part of something larger, a tapestry woven from the city's energy and my own aspirations. Every moment on that road was a reminder of the journey I had embarked on, the challenges I had overcome, and the strength I had found within myself.

The streetlights cast long shadows, their beams reflecting off the smooth surface of the road, creating a dance of light and shadow that was mesmerizing to watch. As I sped down the road, the lights flickered past me, each one a fleeting reminder of the city's warmth, a silent witness to the joy of the ride. The reflections off nearby buildings created a surreal effect, as if the city itself was moving alongside me, a companion on this journey of self-discovery.

The road ahead stretched out like a ribbon of light, each intersection, each roundabout a new chapter, a new adventure waiting to be embraced. The headlights of passing cars created a symphony of light, their beams crossing paths with mine in a beautiful choreography that felt almost poetic. There was a grace to it, a fluidity that echoed the movements of my own journey, a reminder that life, like the road, was a series of moments strung together, each one as fleeting and precious as the last.

There was a strength in the quietness of the night, a confidence that came from embracing the solitude of the ride. The noise of the day had faded, replaced by a stillness that was both comforting and empowering. It was a reminder that strength wasn't always loud or visible—it could be found in the quiet moments, in the spaces between breaths, in the gentle hum of the engine beneath me.

Riding through Gachibowli at night allowed me to tap into that quiet strength, to find power in the silence, to embrace the stillness as a source of resilience. It was a reminder that I didn't need validation from the world around me—the road was enough, the journey was enough, and I was enough.

The road was more than just a path; it was a mirror, reflecting back the journey I had taken, the choices I had made, the person I had become. Riding through the city, feeling the wind against my skin, the hum of the engine beneath me, I felt a sense of clarity, a deep understanding of who I was and who I wanted to be.

Each mile was a reminder of the challenges I had faced, the obstacles I had overcome, the courage it had taken to embrace my true self. The road became a symbol of that courage, a testament to the strength that had carried me through. It was a reminder that life, like the ride, was about movement, about embracing the journey, about finding joy in the path, not just the destination.

As I continued down the road, I felt a profound sense of gratitude, a quiet appreciation for the journey, for the people who had supported me, for the city that had become my home. This ride, this night, was a celebration of that journey, a moment to honor the path that had brought me here, to embrace the future that awaited.

The road stretched out before me, open and inviting, a blank canvas on which to paint the next chapter of my life. With each mile, each turn, each breath, I felt more alive, more connected, more at peace with myself and the world around me.

In that moment, I knew that this journey was far from over. The road, like life, was filled with endless possibilities, each one waiting to be discovered, to be embraced, to be celebrated. And as I rode through the city, feeling the strength of the night around me, I knew that I was ready for whatever lay ahead

Skater Dress & Biker Boots

It wasn't just any day; it was a day for daring. I decided to wear the skater dress I had eyed in my closet countless times, the one that symbolized confidence and freedom. It was a floral aqua blue piece, fitted at the waist with a flare that gently floated around me. This dress felt like an embodiment of everything I had worked to accept in myself—the femininity I had embraced, the boldness I was nurturing, and the desire to ride my bike without compromise, blending strength and elegance in a way that felt like poetry.

As I stood before the mirror, adjusting the soft fabric and making sure the fit was just right, a part of me hesitated. Could I really pull this off? Riding a bike in a skater dress wasn't exactly conventional; it wasn't the usual jeans-and-jacket outfit. But then again, wasn't that the point? To define my own style, to break the boundaries of convention, to create my own version of what it meant to be a lady biker?

The long black boots completed the look, grounding me with an edge that balanced the soft lines of the dress. As I slipped on my helmet and pulled the visor down, I felt like a character from an urban legend, a figure who belonged on these streets but brought a story of their own. I knew this ride was going to be different—it was a moment to fully own my presence, to be seen, to be unapologetically me.

As I mounted the bike, the cool leather of the seat felt grounding, reminding me of the familiar thrill of the road ahead. The skirt of the dress settled neatly around me as I adjusted my position, feeling a small rush of excitement as I pressed onto the start button bringing the engine to life. The first few moments were exhilarating; the hum of the bike beneath me, the fabric of the dress lightly brushing my thighs, and the air, cool and refreshing, hitting my face through the helmet vents.

As I rolled down the street, I could feel the eyes of people passing by. Some were admiring, others curious, a few surprised, and all of them watching as I rode with confidence. A part of me felt like a trailblazer, like I was breaking down the invisible barriers of what a biker should look like or wear. Each look from a passerby, each admiring nod, only fuelled my confidence, making me sit a little straighter, ride a little smoother, and smile a little wider behind the visor.

The wind danced with the fabric of the dress as I rode, creating a sensation of freedom that extended beyond the physical. It felt like a metaphor for the journey I was on—a journey of embracing the feminine power within me, of riding through life with both grace and strength, of defying expectations and creating my own path.

Stopping at a red light, I felt the attention even more acutely. Cars lined up beside me, and I could see drivers and passengers sneaking glances, some subtly, others openly staring in admiration or surprise. One of them, a young woman in the passenger seat of a nearby car, offered a thumbs-up with a bright smile. I returned her smile, feeling a silent camaraderie, a shared moment of acknowledgment that didn't need words.

At that moment, the city felt like a stage, each street and traffic stop an opportunity to express myself, to be seen as the woman I was becoming. There was a quiet thrill in these exchanges, a mutual appreciation that went beyond words, as if the road itself had become a canvas on which I was painting my story. The admiration from strangers felt validating, a reminder that I wasn't just riding for myself; I was also challenging perceptions, showing that strength and femininity could coexist, harmoniously and beautifully.

Riding in a dress was a new experience in itself, and it required a certain balance, a certain grace that added another layer to the ride. I learned quickly how to position myself to ensure the dress stayed secure, to let the wind flow through the fabric without disrupting my focus or comfort. There was a certain art to it, a dance of movement and stillness, a way of riding that allowed me to feel the freedom of the dress without losing control.

The boots, too, added to the experience, their weight grounding me, reminding me of the strength that resided in both the bike and myself. They provided a sense of security, a reminder that while I embraced femininity, there was a powerful edge that couldn't be ignored. Riding in this outfit was more than just a choice of style—it was an expression, a way of saying that femininity was as fierce as it was graceful.

As I sped down the street, I could feel the reactions from pedestrians and other riders. Some nodded in admiration, others smiled, and a few gave double-takes, their expressions a blend of surprise and appreciation. I was fully aware of the impact my presence had, not just as a biker but as a woman who chose to ride her way, unbound by conventions or expectations.

There were moments when I passed groups of young girls, their eyes lighting up as they saw me ride by. In their expressions, I could see a spark of inspiration, a sense of possibility that maybe, just maybe, they too could embrace whatever identity, whatever passion, they chose. It was a powerful feeling, knowing that my ride could be a symbol of freedom, not just for myself but for others.

Riding through Hyderabad in my skater dress and boots was a moment of profound empowerment. The city, with its chaotic traffic and unpredictable roads, had often felt intimidating, especially in the beginning. But tonight, with the lights of Gachibowli reflecting off the chrome of my bike, I felt like I owned the road. It was a feeling of both strength and grace, a blend that resonated deeply with me, as if I was reclaiming every moment of self-doubt, every hesitation, every uncertainty.

Each stretch of road felt like an affirmation, a reminder of the resilience I had cultivated, the courage it took to fully embrace who I was. The bike beneath me, the boots that hugged my legs, the dress that flowed with the wind—it all came together to create a sense of wholeness, a feeling that I was exactly where I needed to be, exactly who I was meant to be.

Not everyone on the road was respectful or admiring. Hyderabad's roads were also home to a few *chapri* riders—those with flashy bikes and louder personalities, who often treated the streets as their own playground, without helmets and road discipline. Infact, they exist not just in Hyderabad but anywhere and everywhere! As I waited at a stoplight, one of these riders pulled up beside me, revving his engine loudly, clearly trying to catch my attention. I could feel his gaze, his attempt to impress or intimidate.

But instead of feeling daunted, I felt a sense of calm confidence wash over me. I held my ground, ignoring his antics, my focus steady on the road ahead. When the light turned green, I accelerated smoothly, leaving him behind without a second glance. It wasn't about proving anything to him or anyone else—it was about proving to myself that I had nothing to prove. My presence, my ride, my confidence, was enough.

As I continued down the road, I felt a wave of satisfaction settle over me. This ride wasn't just about breaking stereotypes; it was about fully embracing the woman I had become, the confidence I had nurtured, and the journey that had led me here. Riding in a skater dress, with boots and a helmet, I was a living contradiction to the old rules and limitations, a blend of strength and elegance that felt uniquely mine.

There was a peace in knowing that I could be both—a biker with a passion for the road, and a woman unafraid to flaunt her style, her confidence, her individuality. Each mile, each turn, each stop was a reminder that femininity was powerful, that riding a bike wasn't just an act of strength but an expression of beauty, of grace, of resilience.

As I neared home, the city quieting around me, I took a moment to reflect on the ride, the freedom, and the sense of self I had found along the way. Riding in a dress, feeling the admiring glances, holding my ground against the occasional rude rider—it all felt like part of a larger story, a journey that was far from over. I was learning to balance elegance with strength, style with substance, grace with grit.

The streets of Hyderabad had seen my transformation, my journey from hesitation to confidence, from self-doubt to self-assurance. This ride, this night, felt like a celebration, not just of who I was but of the power of embracing the road as my own.

The Art of Riding in Style & Confidence

Before every ride, I would pause by my wardrobe, carefully selecting an outfit that would capture the spirit of the journey ahead. Riding had become more than just an activity—it was an art, an expression of my identity, and a celebration of everything I had worked so hard to embrace. The process of choosing the right outfit was like preparing for a performance, each piece adding to the persona I wanted to embody that day. More than making a statement, I wanted myself to feel best from within. It was not competing with others, but competing with myself, my present self, to be the better version of me, every time!

Some days, I would reach for the classic look: fitted jeans, a comfortable top, and my jacket, a symbol of resilience and adventure. Other days, a softer, more elegant look felt fitting, especially if the ride was more reflective or leisurely. These choices weren't just about practicality—they were about embracing who I was, blending strength and femininity into one cohesive style.

My wardrobe had transformed into a collection of pieces that each told a part of my story. The jeans, sturdy and reliable, represented the grounded strength I had built within myself. The tops, each with their own unique style, were a nod to the individuality I was embracing. The jacket, with its worn edges, stuck on patches from my old riding days and classic cut, was a tribute to the biker culture that had welcomed me so openly.

There was something empowering about dressing intentionally for a ride. Each layer, each accessory, added to the confidence I felt as I prepared to hit the road. One of my favourite outfits for longer rides was a simple, well-fitted top paired with dark jeans and ankle boots. It was comfortable, yet stylish, and allowed me to move with ease while still feeling presentable if I decided to stop at a cafe or a friend's place.

The boots were an essential part of my riding attire. They were sturdy, offering both protection and a sense of groundedness. As I laced them up, I felt a sense of purpose; it was like slipping into a version of myself that was bold, confident, and unafraid to take on whatever the day had in store. The boots were a reminder that I was a woman who knew her way around a bike, who could handle the challenges of the road with both grace and grit.

Every time I completed an outfit with my favourite riding jacket, I felt an undeniable sense of readiness. The jacket, a classic blue *Cramster* piece with a sleek fit, was more than just a piece of clothing—it was a piece of armour, a symbol of my commitment to the journey, a reminder of the strength I had cultivated. Sliding my arms into it felt like donning a second skin, one that held stories of past rides, of victories over self-doubt, and of the road that lay ahead.

One of my boldest choices was the skater dress—a departure from the classic biker look, and a statement that was uniquely me. The dress was a soft, flowing piece in a floral aqua blue, a colour that felt both grounding and elegant. When I first tried it on for a ride, there was a thrill in the unfamiliarity of it, a sense of excitement in stepping beyond the traditional attire.

Riding in a dress was more than a fashion choice—it was an assertion of the femininity I had embraced, a way of saying that I didn't have to fit into a particular mold to be a biker. The skater dress, with its gentle flare and comfortable fit, allowed me to ride with a sense of freedom that felt both powerful and graceful. It was a reminder that my identity as a rider wasn't defined by conventions but by my own choices.

Every time I stopped at a traffic light or parked the bike, I could feel the eyes of onlookers, their expressions a mix of admiration and surprise. There was a sense of pride in knowing that I was challenging perceptions, that I was redefining what it meant to be a woman on a bike. The dress wasn't just clothing—it was a part of the journey, a celebration of the woman I was becoming.

Riding, especially in Hyderabad's unpredictable weather, required a thoughtful selection of fabrics and accessories. Over time, I learned the importance of choosing breathable, flexible fabrics that allowed for ease of movement. Cotton tops were a favourite for warmer days, providing comfort and a soft touch against the skin, while thicker fabrics like denim or leather provided added protection and durability.

Accessories became both functional and expressive. A simple scarf, for instance, added a pop of colour and personality to an otherwise simple outfit. It was a practical choice, too, providing warmth on cooler rides or a shield against dust on long stretches. Each accessory, whether a pair of gloves or a stylish belt, reflected my personality, an element that contributed to the unique style I was creating.

One of my most cherished accessories was a pair of fingerless gloves, a blend of leather and fabric that offered both protection and a touch of elegance, only to be used in city rides, although they offer limited to no protection. Every time I slipped them on, I felt a connection to the tradition of biking, a nod to the culture that had welcomed me, and a reminder of the journey I was on.

Practicality was an essential consideration, especially for longer rides. The outfits I chose needed to offer both comfort and protection, ensuring that I could ride for hours without feeling restricted. But there was also a deep sense of satisfaction in finding pieces that combined both function and style. Each outfit became a reflection of my journey, a testament to the balance I was finding between the expectations of the world and the freedom I was discovering within myself.

Some days, I would choose a fitted top with a subtle pattern, pairing it with jeans that hugged my form comfortably, a blend of femininity and practicality that felt true to who I was. The addition of a belt, a pair of gloves, or a scarf brought character to the look, allowing me to express my individuality without compromising on comfort.

Dressing for a ride was more than just an act of preparation—it was a way of embracing the feminine power that I had grown to love. The clothes I wore became a statement, a declaration that I could be both elegant and fierce, graceful and resilient. There was a thrill in knowing that I was breaking boundaries, that I was redefining what it meant to be a woman on a bike.

Riding through the city in an outfit that felt uniquely mine, I felt an incredible sense of empowerment. It wasn't just about being seen—it was about being true to myself, about celebrating the journey that had led me here. The freedom of the ride, combined with the confidence of my chosen style, created a sense of wholeness, a feeling that I was exactly where I was meant to be.

The stares, the admiring glances, the occasional nod of approval—they all became part of the experience, a reflection of the impact my presence had. It was a reminder that femininity was a powerful force, one that could coexist with the strength and resilience that riding demanded. Every mile, every turn, every moment on the road was a testament to that power, a celebration of the journey I was on.

As I rode through the city, feeling the wind against my skin, the hum of the engine beneath me, and the comfort of my chosen outfit, I felt a profound sense of gratitude. Each ride was a reminder of the resilience I had cultivated, the strength I had found within myself, and the courage it had taken to embrace my true self.

The road ahead was open, a blank canvas waiting to be filled with new experiences, new adventures, and new expressions of self. I knew that the journey was far from over, that there were countless more rides to take, more outfits to wear, more moments to embrace. And as I looked ahead, I felt a quiet confidence, a sense of peace that came from knowing that I was exactly where I needed to be, fully present in the moment, fully committed to the journey.

In that moment, I knew that I was more than just a biker, more than just a woman on the road. I was a force, a presence, a story that was still unfolding, and I was ready to embrace every mile, every turn, every challenge that lay ahead.

Curious Eyes at The Petrol Pump

The moment I pulled up to the petrol pump one evening, I could feel the hum of energy around me shift. Even with my helmet still on, the skater dress and long black boots were enough to draw curious glances. The fluorescent lights above illuminated the scene, casting a soft glow over everything, highlighting the gloss of my bike and the sleek lines of my dress. I could see attendants pausing in mid-motion, their heads turning just slightly as they noticed the unique sight of a woman biker dressed in what was undeniably a striking and unusual riding outfit.

Riding in a skater dress was more than just a style choice; it was a celebration of confidence, femininity, and strength. It was about breaking out of the mold and embracing a look that represented who I was. I had chosen the dress that evening for its comfort and its statement. It was an outfit that felt like me, and the bike beneath me seemed to share in the pride of that expression.

As I brought my bike to a stop, an attendant nearby dropped what he was doing, his wide eyes taking in the sight of a woman biker in full gear but with an unconventional twist. His expression made me smile behind the visor. This was one of the beautiful things about riding—each stop, each interaction, was a chance to show the world that bikers come in all forms, and that there's no one way to look or dress on the road.

At a petrol pump, as I removed my helmet, I felt the cool evening air against my face, refreshing after the warmth of the ride. I caught the eye of the young attendant as he approached. His expression was a mix of awe, respect, and curiosity, his face lighting up with a barely-contained grin. He paused for a second, seemingly collecting his thoughts, before finally speaking up.

"Madam," he said, unable to hide the amusement in his tone, "you're riding in that dress?"
His question wasn't judgmental—it was genuine curiosity mixed with admiration. I laughed, a sound that seemed to put him at ease, and handed him the payment.
"Yes, it's surprisingly comfortable!" I replied, enjoying the look of surprise and respect in his eyes. "The bike doesn't care what I'm wearing as long as I know how to ride it well."

My answer seemed to amuse him, and his grin widened. Around us, a few people looked up from their cars or bikes, clearly curious about the exchange. There was an energy in the air, a sense of shared appreciation for the unexpected, and I could feel a silent camaraderie forming, as if my presence had broken the routine of their evening, adding a touch of excitement.

A few more people began to take notice. Some simply nodded in appreciation, while others smiled or whispered to one another, clearly intrigued. Among them, a young woman stepped forward, her expression one of admiration and curiosity. Her gaze was fixed on my boots, her eyes lighting up as she took in the outfit, clearly drawn to the combination of strength and style.

“Those boots are amazing,” she said, her voice warm and genuine. “Where did you get them?”
I smiled, happy to share. “Thank you! I got them a while back—they’re my go-to for riding. Comfortable and sturdy, and they go with just about anything.”

Our brief conversation felt like a spark of connection, a shared appreciation for fashion and confidence. She nodded, clearly impressed, and for a moment, I felt as though I was sharing a small piece of my story with her—a story of embracing self-expression, of breaking stereotypes, of riding with both style and strength. It was a reminder that riding wasn’t just about reaching a destination; it was about connecting with people, sharing moments that were both simple and profound.

As I waited for the tank to fill, I took a moment to observe the people around me. Some were still stealing glances, their expressions a mix of surprise and admiration. I noticed a group of young men in a car nearby, clearly curious about the sight of a woman biker dressed in such an unconventional way. They exchanged looks, whispering to one another, but their expressions held no malice—just intrigue and a hint of respect.

In another car, a family was gathered, their children pressing their faces against the window to get a better look. The mother offered me a nod and a smile, a gesture that felt both approving and kind. It was a small moment, but it held a warmth that made me feel seen and accepted. These glances, these smiles, were subtle but powerful, a reminder that the road was a space for everyone, and that each of us had the right to define what it meant to be a biker.

Standing there, surrounded by curious onlookers and friendly faces, I felt a surge of pride. This wasn't just a pit stop to refuel—it was a moment of visibility, a chance to represent a new narrative in the world of biking. It was a reminder that I didn't have to fit into a particular mold to be a rider, that I could bring my own style, my own identity, to the road.

There was a sense of empowerment in knowing that my presence was challenging perceptions, that I was showing people a different side of what it meant to be a biker. It was an affirmation of the journey I had taken, the courage it had taken to embrace my true self, to ride with both confidence and grace. Each smile, each nod, felt like a quiet acknowledgment, a recognition that the road belonged to all of us, regardless of how we looked or dressed.

As I finished paying, another woman approached, her expression a mix of admiration and curiosity. She looked at me for a moment, as if gathering her thoughts, before finally speaking.
"I just wanted to say—you look amazing," she said, her voice warm and genuine. "I've never seen a woman ride like this, especially not in a dress. It's inspiring."

Her words touched me, and I could feel a surge of gratitude for the connection we were sharing. "Thank you," I replied, my voice filled with appreciation. "I think it's important to ride in a way that feels true to who we are, no matter what that looks like. Biking isn't just about fitting in—it's about expressing ourselves, and feeling free."

She nodded, clearly moved, and for a moment, we stood there in shared understanding. It was a small conversation, but it held a weight that felt meaningful, a reminder that each ride was an opportunity to inspire, to connect, to show people that there was no one way to be a biker.

As I put my helmet back on, I could still feel the eyes of the crowd, their expressions filled with a mix of admiration and respect. I offered a final wave, a gesture of gratitude for the warmth and acceptance I had felt, and revved the engine, the familiar hum filling the air. There was a sense of closure as I prepared to leave, a feeling that this brief stop had become something more—a moment of connection, a chance to share a piece of my journey with strangers who, in their own way, had become part of the story.

As I pulled away from the pump, I could see some of them watching me go, their faces still turned toward the bike, their expressions thoughtful, admiring. It was a reminder that each ride, each stop, was an opportunity to show the world the diversity and strength of bikers, to challenge expectations and embrace the freedom of self-expression.

As I rode away from the petrol pump, the night unfolding around me, I felt a deep sense of purpose. This stop had been more than just a chance to refuel—it had been a moment of visibility, a reminder that every choice I made on the road was a testament to my journey, my identity, my strength. Riding wasn't just about the destination—it was about embracing each moment, each interaction, as a part of the journey.

With the city lights stretching ahead, I felt a sense of excitement, a quiet confidence that reminded me of the road's potential. There was still so much to explore, so many rides to take, so many people to connect with. And in that moment, I knew that this journey was far from over—that each ride, each conversation, would continue to shape the story I was creating, one mile, one moment, one connection at a time.

Seeking Safe Spaces

The freedom of the road is exhilarating, but for women riders, that freedom comes with a subtle edge of caution. The vastness, while inviting, also has undercurrents of vulnerability—an awareness that safety isn't a given but a responsibility, a burden that must be constantly shouldered. Each ride brings a new wave of excitement but also a familiar blend of caution, a balancing act between the thrill of the journey and the knowledge that not every stop is a safe one.

On one memorable trip to Hampi recently, the road stretched out in a ribbon of solitude, framed by green fields and small clusters of houses. The ride was peaceful, almost meditative, until the moment I slowed down for a brief rest stop. A small roadside tea stall seemed like the perfect place to pause, but as I dismounted, I felt the weight of several eyes on me—men sitting in a nearby truck, sipping tea and watching me intently.

There was nothing overtly threatening in their gaze, yet the quiet judgment in their eyes was unmistakable. They didn't have to say a word; the feeling of being out of place, of not belonging, was palpable. I took a deep breath, reminded myself why I loved the road, and continued my stop, determined not to let the gaze of strangers rob me of the joy of my ride.

These moments are a quiet struggle, a reminder that freedom often comes with compromises. While I longed to sit and enjoy my tea in peace, the need to be vigilant tempered the experience. It's a familiar paradox—embracing the vastness of the road while remaining constantly aware of the unseen boundaries that society has drawn.

Not every stop carries this tension. Some places offer a rare, comforting sense of welcome—a "safe space" amidst the expanse of the road. I found out a specific café within Hyderabad that became a regular stop after my weekend rides, *Garage Moto Cafe*. It had a wonderful ambience calling out the bikers and every item placed there was curated perfectly to create the biker's ambience. The staff recognized me after a few visits, always greeted me with warm smiles. There was a corner table by the open space, where I would sit, sip on my chai, and watch the world pass by.

In that small café, I could relax fully, my helmet resting in a corner, knowing I wouldn't be judged or interrupted. It was a reminder that safe spaces don't always have to be created; sometimes, they find you. Over time, this little café became more than just a pit stop—it was a sanctuary, a place where I could unwind, reflect on my journey, and feel at home.

For women riders, finding these pockets of safety is like finding hidden gems on a map. Me being a transwoman, it was a bigger thing for me to find such a place! They're rare, but when discovered, they add a richness to the journey that goes beyond the physical miles travelled.

Every ride requires a mental map of potential stops, a calculation of distance, time, and environment. A solo ride becomes a mix of planning and intuition, especially when it comes to identifying stops that feel right. Sometimes, it's not the place itself but the timing. Stopping during daylight feels different from stopping as the sun dips below the horizon, casting shadows that blur the line between safety and risk.

On a ride to Goa, just before entering Karwar, still short of Goa by around 150 kms, night began to fall, and I found myself debating a stop at a small dhaba. My muscles were aching, and I could have used a rest, but the dim lighting and the absence of other women made me pause. I decided to push on, ignoring the fatigue, driven by a sense of caution that had become almost instinctual. Thankfully I had refuelled the tank to sustain me till Karwar. The whole stretch upto Karwar was a Reserve Forest, had no street lights, no road dividers, just passing traffic which was usually big trucks and no suitable stops.

This constant need to evaluate each stop takes a toll, adding a layer of exhaustion that goes beyond the physical. It's a mental load that female riders carry—a silent burden that weighs down the lightness of the road, making every mile both an act of resilience and a victory.

Sometimes, in unexpected places, I would meet fellow travellers—other women, families, or friendly faces—that would shift the tone of a stop entirely. On one occasion, while stopped at a petrol station in Goa, I met a lady who got down from the back seat of a car and walked up to me and conveyed how happy she was to see a woman riding a bike! I smiled at her and told her that I was a transwoman. She said "You're a woman too"! We laughed, exchanged stories, and for a brief moment, the road felt like a shared journey. These connections, however fleeting, reminded me that while the road could be isolating, it was also a place where camaraderie and support could be found in the most unexpected corners.

Each encounter like this added a sense of solidarity, a reminder that I wasn't alone. Other women were out there, navigating their own roads, overcoming their own hurdles, and sharing in the quiet joys and challenges of the journey.

Years of riding have sharpened my instincts, teaching me when to trust a place and when to keep moving. This intuition isn't something that came naturally; it was honed through countless stops, each one a learning experience in reading the environment, assessing people, and gauging my own comfort.

Once, on a longer ride through Madhya Pradesh, I spotted a beautifully quiet rest stop between Gwalior and Agra. The surroundings seemed peaceful, with birds chirping and a soft breeze stirring the trees. But as I approached, something felt off—an inexplicable sense of unease that made me second-guess my choice. Trusting my intuition, I decided to move on, finding a better stop an hour down the road. Later, I heard from another rider that the original spot was known for frequent roadside incidents.

This chapter of my journey is a testament to the power of intuition, the understanding that safety isn't just about the physical surroundings but also about trusting the silent signals our minds give us. Each ride has refined this instinct, teaching me that sometimes, the best choice is to keep moving, to trust that another safe haven lies just around the bend.

Riding has given me a sense of freedom, but the challenges I've faced on the road have inspired a new dream: a network of safe, women-friendly stops across highways, designed with our unique needs in mind. These rest stops could offer clean, accessible bathrooms, secure parking, and a quiet, comfortable space for women riders to rest and recharge without fear or discomfort.

The idea began as a wishful thought, a vision sparked by each challenging stop along my journey. But over time, I've realized that it's not just a dream—it's a necessity, a change that could transform the road for every woman who rides. These safe spaces would redefine the journey, allowing women to embrace the road without compromise.

For now, each ride continues to carry the quiet challenge of finding safe spaces. Yet, with each mile, I hold onto the hope that one day, these stops will be commonplace—a part of every woman's map, a place where safety, comfort, and freedom intersect. Till then, I continue to carry use and throw seat covers for toilets, sanitisers and pepper spray!

Dhabas, India's iconic roadside eateries, are popular with travelers and truck drivers alike, offering quick, affordable meals. But for women riders, dhabas can be an intimidating choice. The spaces are usually crowded with male patrons, and the seating is often out in the open, with little privacy. This reality turns what could be a moment of respite into a test of confidence and comfort.

Once, on a ride with a few friends, we stopped at a dhaba that was known for its chai. While the men in my group settled in comfortably, I felt a familiar hesitation. Every move, from taking off my helmet to adjusting my hair, felt observed. The male patrons didn't mean harm, but their lingering stares were enough to make me feel out of place. Even as I enjoyed the chai, the tension in the air lingered, a subtle reminder that certain spaces weren't designed with us in mind.

I've often found myself balancing between my desire to stop and rest and the unspoken pressure to keep moving, to find a place where I won't stand out. This constant negotiation can be mentally taxing, a reminder of the extra layer of caution that women riders carry with them on every journey.

After numerous uncomfortable stops, I discovered that small cafés often provide a more welcoming environment. Unlike dhabas, which are open-air and informal, cafés offer a degree of privacy and comfort that can make all the difference. Finding these "hidden gems" on the road has become one of my favorite parts of planning a ride. One weekend, while riding through Pune, I stumbled upon a quaint café tucked away from the main highway. The atmosphere was calm, with gentle music and comfortable seating by large windows. I parked my bike, walked in, and felt immediately at ease. The staff was friendly, and I could take my time, enjoying a coffee without any interruptions. This café became a small oasis—a reminder that there are places that make the road feel more inclusive.

These small, women-friendly stops add joy to the ride, transforming the experience from one of endurance into one of true enjoyment. It's in these moments that I feel the potential for change on the road, for more spaces that cater to female travelers.

Fuel stops are essential, but they come with their own set of challenges. Most fuel stations along highways are bustling places, filled with travelers, truck drivers, and employees. While refueling is usually quick, it's not uncommon to feel a sense of unease, particularly when there's no designated area to park the bike safely and rest briefly.

During a solo trip to Bengaluru, I pulled into a petrol pump late in the afternoon. After filling up, I wanted to take a brief break before continuing, but there was no place to sit, no shade, and a few curious eyes that made me think twice about lingering. The lack of facilities and comfort at these essential stops is a common frustration, and it's one that can turn a simple pit stop into a moment of vulnerability.
In that instance, I opted to carry on, knowing I'd have to wait until a more suitable rest spot appeared further along the route. These fuel stops are reminders that, as women, we often make split-second decisions about our safety and comfort, calculating each pause with an added layer of caution.

Rest areas are increasingly available along major highways, but they don't always provide the comfort or privacy that women riders need. While some rest stops are designed with families and women in mind, others lack the essentials—clean bathrooms, shaded seating, or secure parking areas. One night ride to Chandigarh, required a stop at a well-lit rest area. I was grateful to find a place that seemed secure, with designated seating and clean bathrooms. However, despite the basic amenities, the area felt exposed. I found myself sitting in the farthest corner, hoping to stay unnoticed while still enjoying the brief break.

These stops are often a compromise; while they offer the basics, they lack the warmth or privacy needed to feel fully relaxed. For women riders, rest areas are often only as good as the level of comfort they provide, a subtle but important distinction that many overlook.

The challenges of finding safe, comfortable places to stop have often led me to imagine an ideal world for women riders. What if highways featured designated “women-friendly” or “all inclusive” rest stops, designed with our specific needs in mind? These spaces would have secure, shaded seating, clean bathrooms, and perhaps even small café-like setups where riders could enjoy a coffee without the watchful eyes of strangers.

This vision isn’t just a fantasy—it’s a real need, one that would make the road more inclusive for everyone. By creating these spaces, we could redefine what it means to travel as a woman, allowing female riders to embrace the road without compromise or discomfort.

For now, each stop remains a careful decision with my pepper spray in reach, each pause a small act of resilience with the paper toilet seats ready. But with each ride, I hold on to the hope that one day, these challenges will be met with solutions, that the road will truly become a place of freedom for all.

Physical Toll on a Unique Body

Riding long distances challenges every part of the body, but as a transwoman, my experience carries nuances that differ from those of cisgender women riders. While hormone therapy has aligned my body more closely with theirs, I retain certain physical advantages from before my transition that impact my riding experience. This chapter delves into the journey of understanding these differences, embracing my body's unique attributes, and adapting to long-distance rides.

Hormone therapy reshaped my body to an extent, creating a balance between softness and strength that's unique to my experience. Over time, I've developed the curves and contours typical of women, and my skin's sensitivity to touch and temperature has increased, often requiring extra adjustments for comfort on the road. However, I still have the muscle memory and strength from before my transition, giving me an edge in handling the physical demands of biking.

This blend has proven to be both a challenge and an advantage. The muscle strength in my arms and shoulders often allows me to handle the weight of my bike more easily, especially when maneuvering it during stops or tight turns.

Yet, my skin's newfound sensitivity—one of the effects of estrogen—means that the vibrations from the seat and handlebars can cause soreness or even slight bruising during longer rides. Managing both sides of this coin has required patience, adaptation, and a deeper understanding of how to care for my body on the road.

Riding comfort is critical for anyone, but for me, finding a balance between strength and sensitivity has led to more tailored solutions. While my upper body strength helps in controlling the bike, I've found that the lower body needs extra cushioning, especially as my shape has shifted over time. A thicker, gel-based seat cover became a game-changer initially, reducing the impact on my hips and lower back, which have grown more sensitive. Later, over the course of time, I shifted back to the regular seat.

At the same time, certain protective gear, like gloves and jackets, needs to be fitted specifically to avoid pressure on areas where skin sensitivity has increased. On the long ride to Hampi, I tested a new pair of padded gloves, which initially felt too bulky but eventually provided much-needed relief from vibrations. These adjustments, though simple, transformed my riding experience from a constant negotiation with discomfort to a more harmonious journey.

Each ride taught me something new about my body's evolving needs, reminding me that every adjustment brought me closer to a balance between strength and comfort. My core strength has remained one of my greatest assets. Pre-transition, my torso and core muscles developed differently, and while estrogen therapy has softened some of these areas, the underlying strength allows me to navigate my bike with relative ease. This advantage became particularly evident during long stretches or rough patches on the road, where a steady core can make all the difference.

During a ride to the Western Ghats, I hit an unexpectedly bumpy road. With every jolt, I relied on my core to keep my posture stable, preventing excessive strain on my lower back. It's during these moments that I'm grateful for the muscle memory I carry—an advantage that, while subtle, adds to my sense of control on the bike.

However, this doesn't mean I'm immune to fatigue. The physical strain still accumulates, particularly in my legs and lower back, which tend to bear the brunt of the ride. Moreover, handling a heavy bike also takes toll on my shoulders and arms, which have lost mass over the course of hormone therapy. Knowing my strengths helps me approach each challenge with more awareness, but it doesn't exempt me from the toll that every mile takes on my body.

While my body retains certain pre-transition strengths, the effects of hormone therapy have brought new challenges. Over time, my body fat distribution has changed, leading to softer tissue around my hips and thighs, areas that are more prone to soreness on long rides. I've had to adjust my seating position and learn how to relieve pressure on these sensitive areas, especially during extended journeys.

During one memorable to the nearby hills, the incline and winding roads required constant shifting of weight, which began to strain my legs. By the time I reached a rest stop, my hips were sore from the constant pressure. I realized then that my body's structure now called for more frequent breaks and careful weight distribution to manage the strain. I realised, how easy it was for my body before to negotiate such problems during long rides.

This chapter of my riding experience taught me to listen more closely to my body, understanding that the balance between strength and sensitivity is one I must honor. It's a blend of embracing my femininity while acknowledging the strengths I carry forward from before my transition.

Riding long distances became a lesson in endurance, not just of the road but of my own evolving body. Every ride challenged my resilience, teaching me how to adapt to changes, be it in posture, gear, or mindset. Each ache and strain became a message from my body, reminding me that comfort isn't just about physical adjustments; it's about embracing the transformation that each mile brings.

After a particularly strenuous ride to Shimla, I noticed my body's resilience in a new way. My shoulders, though sore, had held up well against the weight of my jacket and helmet. My legs, despite the discomfort, bore the journey without giving in. And while my hips and lower back needed extra care, they carried the miles as a testament to my body's adaptability.

These rides taught me that resilience is born not from perfection, but from the ability to adapt and grow with each challenge. My body's unique blend of strength and softness slowly became a source of pride, a reminder that every mile is a testament to both who I am and who I'm becoming.

The blend of masculine and feminine attributes in my body has created a riding experience that's uniquely mine. I have the advantage of strength, yet the evolving softness of my body adds new challenges, reminding me that comfort is a journey, not a destination. Learning to balance these aspects has deepened my connection to the road, transforming each ride into a journey of self-discovery.

As I pull off my helmet after a long day's ride, feeling the weight lift and the wind brush against my face, I'm reminded of the balance I've achieved. Each ride is a lesson in honouring my body, adapting to its needs, and celebrating the resilience that allows me to navigate the challenges with grace.

In the end, riding has become more than just a physical journey; it's a reflection of my transition, my growth, and my ability to embrace both strength and sensitivity in equal measure. Every mile is a reminder that comfort, resilience, and adaptability define not only the road but the life I've chosen to live.

Breaking Down Stereotypes

Biking has often been labelled as a masculine pursuit, surrounded by stereotypes that challenge the very idea of women on motorcycles. For me, joining a community of riders wasn't just about hitting the road but about proving to myself—and sometimes others—that biking has no gender. Through shared respect, support, and confidence-building moments, I began to see myself through the eyes of my fellow riders: not as a transwoman or an anomaly, but simply as a biker. In this chapter, I explore how my community's acceptance helped me break down stereotypes and find empowerment on the road.

Even before I joined the biking community, I sensed the quiet judgment that often accompanies women on motorcycles. Riding wasn't just a mode of transport or a hobby; it was a statement of independence. But as a transwoman, I carried an additional layer of expectation. Each time I rode, it felt like an act of defiance against the preconceived notions surrounding gender roles, especially in the conservative corners of society.

In those early days, I often encountered raised eyebrows and whispered comments when I pulled up at events or rode through new areas. Strangers would occasionally offer unsolicited advice on safety or handling, assuming my knowledge was limited by my gender. However, every glance or murmur only fuelled my determination.

Riding wasn't about proving others wrong; it was about proving to myself that I could pursue my passion, regardless of societal expectations. The more I rode with the community, the more I felt the stereotypes begin to dissolve. The bikers around me didn't care about my gender or my background; they respected my commitment to the road. I realized that as much as I was challenging their perceptions, they were challenging mine, teaching me that riding was, at its core, a shared love for adventure and freedom.

One of the first moments that truly shifted my perspective happened during a weekend ride to a quiet hill station. We had all gathered early in the morning, the excitement palpable as engines revved and helmets clicked into place. I was nervous, not about the ride itself, but about how I'd fit in with the group.

It was Vijay, a seasoned rider with years of experience, who first approached me with a friendly nod. As we prepared to set off, he casually remarked, "You're a natural on that bike. I can tell you've got the instincts." His words were simple, but they held a weight that stayed with me throughout the ride.
During one of the stops, he noticed me checking the vitals of the bike – engine oil, belt, brakes, indiators etc, something I'd learned to do meticulously to avoid issues on longer rides. Vijay observed for a moment before speaking.

"Most people don't bother with the basics like that. Shows you care about your bike," he said, his tone filled with approval.

This kind of acknowledgment was empowering. Here was a seasoned rider who respected me not for fitting into any mold, but for my commitment and knowledge. Each ride after that became less about proving myself and more about embracing the journey with a new sense of confidence. Vijay's respect and trust shifted something within me, showing me that my place in this world was earned through passion and dedication.

As my confidence grew, I began to take on more active roles within the group. Leading a segment of a ride or helping plan a route was something I would've shied away from at the beginning. But the respect I had received from my fellow riders gave me the courage to step up.

One day, while going back from the *Flag Ride,* I decided to shift gears and float along the column since I was recording the whole ride on my camera mounted on the bike. I lead, followed and moved as per my instincts.

Leading that ride felt transformative. As I looked in the rearview mirror and saw a line of bikes following my lead, I felt an overwhelming sense of pride. Each turn and decision along the route was a testament to the trust the group had placed in me, a validation that went beyond words.

After the ride, one of the newer riders, who had joined only recently, approached me with a smile.
"I hope to ride as confidently as you someday," she said.

Those words encapsulated everything I'd been working toward. It wasn't just about proving that women could ride; it was about inspiring others to follow their passions without fear. Leadership, I realized, wasn't about perfection but about resilience and the courage to pave the way for others.

I remember having attended a launch of a particular bike at one of the showrooms in Hyderabad, where I met a few girls who were comparatively new to biking. I had come to this launch event straight from my bike trip to Hampi. The girls were fascinated by my stories and I actually felt that I could inspire girls to follow footsteps or even to follow their own biking dreams! It doesn't mean they lacked sef motivation. It signifies the importance of seeing a woman like them already doing things that they want to do, cementing their beliefs that they can do it too or maybe they could do much better and much more!

Over time, the group's respect and camaraderie taught me to see myself differently. I wasn't "the transwoman biker" or "the woman trying to fit in." I was simply a biker. My identity, shaped by experiences on the road, became less about labels and more about shared purpose and connection.

There was one ride to the mountains that felt like a turning point. The path was challenging, with steep inclines and narrow curves. Everyone was focused, pushing their limits, yet supporting each other with gestures and glances that communicated unspoken understanding. In those moments, as I navigated each turn and incline alongside my fellow riders, my identity felt both vast and singular. I wasn't defined by labels; I was a part of something larger, something boundless.

After that ride, I realized that I didn't have to constantly justify my place in the biking world. My fellow riders saw me for my skills, my passion, and my commitment. I was a biker first, a part of a community that transcended individual identities.

As I grew in confidence, I began to see that my presence in the community was making a difference, not just for me but for others who might have felt constrained by similar stereotypes. Friends outside the biking world often expressed surprise and admiration when they saw photos or heard stories of my rides.

One evening, I shared a conversation with Vijeta, reflecting on the journey that had brought us together and the way we both navigated a world where riding was often seen as "too bold" for women.
"You know, every time I see you ride, it feels like a win for all of us and I totally admire you for who you are" she said, her smile filled with warmth.

Her words reminded me of the quiet power that lay in simply being myself. Each mile, each ride, was a statement of defiance against the stereotypes that surrounded women, transwomen, and the biking community. The acceptance I had found in my group wasn't just empowering for me; it was a testament to the power of authenticity in breaking down societal boundaries.

The journey of riding alongside others who respected me for who I was became one of the most empowering experiences of my life. In the company of these riders, I found a resilience that went beyond the physical challenges of the road. Every gesture of acceptance, every shared story, and every mile ridden together built a foundation of trust and strength that sustained me.

One rainy evening, as we huddled under a shelter waiting for the storm to pass, I realized how much these friendships had changed me. Surrounded by people who had seen me at my most vulnerable, who had celebrated my victories and offered support in challenging times, I felt a deep sense of belonging. Each of them had, in their own way, broken down a barrier for me, helping me reclaim the freedom that society had tried to take away.

Breaking down stereotypes wasn't a one-time act; it was a journey of resilience, supported by a community that believed in the power of the road to connect and liberate. Each friendship, each ride, became a reminder that true empowerment comes not from defying labels but from embracing the road with courage, knowing that our strength lies not in fitting in but in standing out.

This chapter celebrates the triumph of self-acceptance, the courage to challenge societal norms, and the invaluable support of a community that valued me for my passion and my spirit. Through the road, I found not only freedom but a purpose—to ride for myself and, in doing so, inspire others to do the same.

The Power of Community Rides

For any biker, the thrill of riding often finds its deepest meaning in the shared experiences of group rides and community events. The sense of unity that comes from riding in formation, the electric energy of a large gathering, and the friendships that form along the way turn the open road into a journey of connection. In this chapter, I dive into some of the most memorable events and group rides that have left a lasting mark on my life, showing me that the road is never truly empty when you ride with others by your side.

There are many cause rides that take place in the city bringing riders from different walks of life, riding different types of bikes together for a common cause or purpose. Such events aren't just about riding; it's about giving back, using our passion for a purpose greater than ourselves. The excitement begins weeks before, as riders start preparing, sharing the event details with friends and family, and inviting as many people as possible to join. Registrations are done and groups start taking the count.

On the morning of one such ride, the air was buzzing with anticipation. The sun was just beginning to rise, casting a warm glow over the sea of motorcycles gathered at the meeting point. I remember seeing every type of bike imaginable—sleek sports bikes, rumbling cruisers, and humble commuters.

In that moment, our differences faded into the background; what united us was a shared purpose and a collective respect for the road. As we set off, the city seemed to awaken with us, watching as a line of riders, united by a common mission, wound through the streets. Each turn, each signal, was a silent nod of solidarity, a reminder that we were more than just individuals on bikes; we were a community, a force for change.

The ride ended with a gathering at a local restaurant, where we celebrated the success of the event with food, music, and speeches from organizers. Waving to children in school buses or bystanders, respecting traffic rules and making a statement while we ride is something which creates a huge impact. It was inspiring to see how many lives our ride could touch, how our collective love for riding could bring about tangible, positive impact. This event taught me that riding wasn't just a solitary pursuit; it was a powerful tool for unity, capable of creating real change in the world.

While larger events like the charity ride and the DGR are impactful, it's often the smaller group rides that forge the deepest connections. These rides, usually organized on a whim, offer a unique blend of camaraderie and adventure, allowing us to explore new places and create memories that stay with us long after the ride is over.

One Sunday morning, *HYDE* planned a breakfast ride to a small Dhaba, just outside the city. The air was crisp, and the roads were quiet, offering the perfect conditions for a relaxed, scenic ride. As we rode, each person settled into their own rhythm, yet we remained connected, a fluid line of bikes weaving through the landscape.

At our destination, after ordering the breakfast, sitting on makeshift stools, sipping hot chai, and chatting about the road ahead, I felt a profound sense of belonging. Conversations ranged from bike modifications to travel stories and future ride plans, each rider bringing their own experiences and perspectives to the table. These moments of shared laughter, support, and encouragement reminded me that the bonds we built on the road were more than just friendships—they were lifelines, connections that deepened with every mile we shared.

After breakfast, we continued our ride, each milestone of the road feeling like a testament to the strength of our community. As we reached back and looked back, I realized that this journey, these shared experiences, had shaped my life in ways I couldn't have anticipated. The road wasn't just a destination; it was a journey of unity, strength, and shared purpose.

Not every ride goes smoothly, and some of the most memorable experiences come from moments when things go wrong. During one group ride to a remote village, one of the bikes unexpectedly broke down. The rider, a relatively new member, looked anxious and unsure about what to do.

Without a second thought, a few riders pulled over to help, inspecting the bike with practiced hands. Others joined in, offering tools, advice, and moral support. The breakdown turned into a spontaneous workshop, with each person contributing their knowledge and skills to get the bike back on the road.

As I watched the group come together, working as a team, I felt an overwhelming sense of gratitude. In these moments, the biker community become a family, each person's safety and success intertwined with the others'. The breakdown was a reminder that the strength of our bond wasn't just in the miles we covered, but in the way we supported each other, especially in times of need.

The bike was eventually fixed, and we continued our ride, laughing about the unexpected detour. The incident brought us closer, turning a potential setback into a powerful memory of resilience, teamwork, and trust. It reminded me that the road, with all its challenges, was a place of growth, where every rider found strength not only in themselves but in the people they rode alongside.

These rides and events didn't just shape my experiences as a rider; they transformed my sense of self. Through each group ride, each community event, I found an empowering support system that celebrated my individuality while also embracing me as part of something larger. The community taught me that the road was a space of freedom, unity, and expression, a place where we could be our truest selves without fear or hesitation.

In a world where I'd often felt defined by labels, the biker community allowed me to reclaim my identity. They saw me not just as a transwoman or an outcast, but as a fellow rider, someone who shared their passion for the road and the love for the journey.

This acceptance went beyond words; it was a respect that showed up in actions, in the shared miles, and in the support we offered each other on and off the bike. At the Rynox event that I attended at the start of my Hyderabad story, a guy named Sreen walked up to me and asked me as to why I had mentioned during my introduction that I was a transwoman. He insisted that, it was not my identity. For others, the only thing that must matter is that I am a rider. That's all!

Being part of the biker community showed me that riding wasn't just an individual pursuit; it was a collective journey, filled with shared moments, laughter, and resilience. Each event, each ride, became a testament to the strength of our bond, a reminder that the road wasn't just about the destination but about the people we shared it with. Through charity rides, the Distinguished Gentleman's Ride, and spontaneous group trips, I found a family of riders who believed in me, supported me, and helped me become the rider—and the person that I am today. This community gave me more than just companionship; it gave me a place to belong, a sense of purpose, and a journey that continues to inspire me with every mile.

Finding Purpose Beyond Road

Through my journey with the biker community, I experienced something truly transformative—a profound growth in my sense of self, a deeper confidence, and a renewed commitment to purpose. This chapter delves into how my interactions, friendships, and experiences within the community shaped not only my riding but also my life. Each person, each ride, taught me valuable lessons that went beyond the miles and brought me closer to who I am and who I want to be.

When I first joined the community, I was searching for a sense of belonging, a place where I could be myself without judgment. Over time, the support and respect I received from my fellow riders helped me grow in ways I hadn't anticipated. Each shared experience, each ride, built my confidence layer by layer, allowing me to embrace my role in the community with pride.

One of the most memorable moments was a solo ride organized by Shweta, who had been instrumental in bringing women bikers together. She invited me to lead a segment of the ride—a role I would've hesitated to take on earlier. But Shweta's unwavering faith in me pushed me forward. As I rode at the front, guiding the group through twists and turns, I felt a newfound strength radiating from within. I wasn't just following; I was leading, and the trust placed in me by my friends fuelled my confidence.

By the time we reached our destination, the encouragement I received from the group made me realize I'd transcended a significant barrier. This was a moment of growth, a reminder that the journey wasn't about proving myself to anyone but about becoming the best version of myself.

The friendships I formed within the community became more than just companionship; they were transformative relationships that encouraged personal growth on a deeper level. Each person, from Shweta to Vijeta and Jacob, taught me something valuable, creating a network of support and understanding that extended beyond the road.
Vijeta, with her quiet wisdom and introspective nature, showed me the beauty of patience and listening. On several rides, she would listen to my problems, calm me down, guiding me through challenging terrain of life while sharing her life stories that left me feeling both empowered and inspired. We spent countless hours sharing our dreams and struggles, realizing that our journeys, though different, were driven by the same desire for freedom and self-expression.

Jacob, too, became a mentor of sorts, someone who encouraged me to explore the technical aspects of riding and maintaining my bike. His knowledge was extensive, and he never hesitated to share it, offering tips and insights that helped me become a more skilled rider. Through him, I learned that resilience and knowledge were my greatest tools on the road.

These friendships weren't just about companionship; they were catalysts for growth, pushing me to step out of my comfort zone, to learn and adapt, and to embrace the person I was becoming.

As my confidence grew, so did my desire to contribute to the community that had given me so much. The idea of giving back took root during one of our charity rides, where I saw the potential of our collective power to make a difference. Riding for a cause, seeing the impact of our efforts, made me realize that biking could be more than just a personal pursuit; it could be a way to bring positive change.

Inspired, I began taking part in small events and rides that focused on awareness and charity. One event, organized with the help of Shweta and other members, aimed to raise awareness about women's safety in India. We partnered with local organizations, spoke at parks, and even planned future workshops on self-defence and bike maintenance for women. Watching people respond with interest and enthusiasm was a moment of pride, a realization that our passion had a purpose beyond the thrill of the ride.

I started mentoring younger riders, too, especially women who were new to the community and unsure of their place. Through casual talks, coffee meetups, and group rides, I shared my journey, hoping to inspire them to follow their passion without fear. Each time I saw a new rider's confidence grow, I felt a renewed sense of purpose, a reminder that our experiences could light the path for others.

Through my journey in the community, I realized that my presence was breaking down stereotypes and inspiring acceptance, both within myself and in those around me. The acceptance I received from the community helped me to redefine my identity, not by labels but by the values I carried with me. I was no longer "just a woman" or "a transwoman biker"; I was a respected member of a vibrant, diverse family of riders.

One poignant moment occurred during a public ride we held to celebrate inclusivity and diversity. Riders from all walks of life participated, representing different backgrounds, cultures, and identities. Seeing myself included among this tapestry of diversity, I felt a surge of pride, a deep sense of belonging that transcended any label or preconception. The ride wasn't just a celebration of bikes; it was a celebration of the community we had built, one that respected each individual for their contributions and strengths.

In the conversations that followed the ride, fellow riders shared stories of their own struggles and journeys. Hearing these stories, seeing the courage and resilience each person carried, made me realize that we were more alike than different. We were all on a journey of self-discovery, of breaking down societal barriers, and of creating spaces where we could truly be ourselves.

The biker community taught me that no challenge was insurmountable when faced with unity and resilience. On several rides, we encountered obstacles—unexpected weather changes, breakdowns, and even disagreements—that could have derailed the journey. But each time, we came together, drawing on each other's strengths and finding solutions that strengthened our bond.

One ride in particular, way back in 2015, a long journey to the mountains, became a test of both our physical and mental endurance. Halfway through the journey, a sudden rainstorm hit, drenching us and making the roads treacherous. While some riders considered turning back, others urged us to continue, supporting each other through the challenges.

James, who had been through his share of tough rides, took charge, organizing us into pairs and assigning each group a specific role—some leading, others covering the rear, and some managing supplies. It was teamwork at its best, a blend of experience, courage, and trust that carried us through the storm. By the time we reached our destination, cold and exhausted but triumphant, we were more than a group of riders; we were a team, a family that had faced adversity together and emerged stronger.

These challenges taught me that resilience wasn't just about personal strength; it was about drawing strength from those around you, embracing the journey as a collective experience.

Over time, the biker community became a mirror, reflecting the person I was becoming. The miles we covered, the experiences we shared, and the support we offered each other helped me uncover a purpose beyond myself. Each ride, each event, was a step toward understanding what I wanted out of life, and who I wanted to be.

One evening, as we gathered for a quiet night ride, a rider over a coffee break, turned to me with a question that lingered long after the ride was over.
"Why do you ride?" she asked, her voice thoughtful. "What does it mean to you?"
I paused, reflecting on the question before answering. "I ride to feel free, to be part of something bigger than myself. It's my way of discovering who I am, of finding purpose."
She smiled, nodding as if she understood. That moment stayed with me, a reminder that the road wasn't just a destination; it was a journey of growth, self-discovery, and empowerment.

Riding had given me more than freedom; it had given me a purpose, a reason to push forward, to grow, and to inspire others to do the same. Through my experiences in the community, I realized that my journey was about more than just myself; it was about creating spaces where others could find the same sense of freedom and belonging that I had discovered.

The biker community became a transformative force in my life, teaching me lessons in resilience, unity, and self-acceptance that went beyond the road. Through shared experiences, friendships, and a deep sense of purpose, I found the strength to embrace my journey, to push past limitations, and to celebrate each mile as a testament to the power of connection.

The road may be long, and the journey challenging, but with the support of my fellow riders, I discovered that no challenge was insurmountable, no barrier too strong, and no dream too distant. Together, we were more than just bikers; we were a family, united by the freedom of the road and the love for the journey.

Rediscovering My Passion for Riding

After years of achievements, challenges, and personal growth, I found myself immersed in the pursuit of new goals: excelling as a pilot, becoming a fitness trainer, participating in pageants, and even writing and publishing my memoir. While each endeavour was fulfilling in its own way, I didn't realize that somewhere along the way, my passion for biking had taken a backseat. It was as if the hum of the engine had faded into the background, replaced by the demands of my evolving career and aspirations.

Yet, as the journey unfolded, I discovered that the love for riding had not disappeared—it had simply gone dormant, waiting for the right moment to resurface. This chapter is about reconnecting with that passion, the unexpected twists that led me back to the open road, and the reminder that sometimes, our truest loves never leave us; they simply wait for us to return.

Life has a way of presenting opportunities that shift our focus, and for a while, my attention veered away from biking. My transition, both personal and professional, brought with it a myriad of new challenges and goals that demanded my time and energy. I found myself dedicating long hours to training as a pilot, a journey that required meticulous planning, resilience, and concentration and discipline.

The thrill of taking to the skies, of mastering the art of flight, felt like a new frontier, a calling that had its own exhilaration and sense of freedom. At the same time, I threw myself into fitness, pageants, and even ghostwriting, channelling my creativity and determination into each new venture. Biking, which had once been my solace, my freedom, began to feel like a distant memory. The motorcycle that had once been my constant companion now sat covered in my sister's garage, a silent reminder of a part of me I thought I'd moved on from.

There were days when I'd glance at old photos of my bike, memories of past journeys flickering across my mind. But between the demands of my career and the excitement of new accomplishments, the thought of returning to the road seemed less like a priority and more like a distant dream.

It wasn't until I relocated to Hyderabad and began to settle into my new routine that I felt a quiet tug, an undeniable longing for the road. It started subtly, as I scrolled through social media, stumbling across images of bikers exploring the rugged landscapes of India. Then I saw posts from *Bikerni Hyderabad*—a group of passionate women bikers who shared a camaraderie and a love for riding that was both inspiring and infectious.

Their posts ignited something within me, a spark that had lain dormant for too long. I imagined myself riding alongside them, feeling the wind on my face, the thrill of the journey, and the freedom that only comes from the open road. This time, the desire felt different—it was stronger, more purposeful, as if the road was calling me back not just as a rider but as the person I had become.

I began researching ways to bring my bike to Hyderabad, rekindling the excitement I once felt every time I started the engine. After reaching out to my sister, we made arrangements to ship the bike. As I waited for it to arrive, I found myself anticipating the feeling of the road beneath me, the familiarity of old routines, and the joy of rediscovering a part of myself that I hadn't realized I missed.

The day my bike arrived was a blend of nostalgia, excitement, and emotion. The crate containing my beloved machine had travelled hundreds of miles, and as the delivery team unloaded it, I felt a rush of memories wash over me. The bike, cushioned by pillows and wrapped in protective material, looked almost regal as it emerged from the wooden crate, like a long-lost friend returning home.

Carefully, I removed the packing materials, my fingers tracing the familiar contours and curves. Reconnecting the battery terminals and filling the fuel tank were rituals that brought me back to the countless hours I'd spent maintaining my bike, treating it with the care and attention it deserved. As I pressed the ignition button and heard the engine roar to life, a wave of emotions hit me—the thrill, the joy, the sense of freedom that only a rider can understand.

In that moment, I realized that biking had never left me; it had simply been waiting, patiently, for me to find my way back. I spent hours that day polishing the bike, inspecting every detail, as if reacquainting myself with an old friend.

With my bike back in my life, I was eager to reconnect with the Hyderabad biking community, to ride alongside others who understood the thrill and freedom of the open road. I reached out to a few clubs and soon found myself joining their meet-ups and rides, rediscovering the joy of group riding.

Getting back into riding wasn't just about reconnecting with my bike; it was about rediscovering the art of riding itself. Over time, I'd grown more attuned to comfort and style, and choosing the right riding gear became an essential part of the experience.

A trip to the Rynox store with Deekshitha introduced me to a new jacket—a blue Cramster that felt like a fitting nod to my past while embracing my present.

The ride back home in my new gear felt symbolic, as if I were reuniting with my past self while stepping confidently into my future. With every ride, I could feel the old instincts returning—the subtle shift of weight around curves, the thrill of acceleration, the way the road seemed to stretch endlessly before me.

Yet, the journey wasn't just a nostalgic return; it was a new beginning, a blend of old memories and fresh adventures. Riding in Hyderabad, exploring new routes and hidden trails, felt like a fresh chapter in my story, a reminder that the road, much like life, always offers something new.

Rediscovering my passion for riding rekindled a sense of purpose, a reminder that life is a journey, meant to be explored and embraced at every turn. Each ride brought a new lesson, a reminder of the resilience, freedom, and joy that biking had always given me. The road, with its twists and turns, its challenges and rewards, mirrored my own journey—a path that was never linear but always meaningful.

Now, as I look towards the future, I'm filled with excitement for the adventures yet to come. With each ride, each mile, I'm reminded that the road is not just a destination but a place of growth, connection, and self-discovery. In reclaiming my love for biking, I've rediscovered a part of myself that fuels my spirit, and I know that no matter where life takes me, the road will always be there, waiting to welcome me back.

The Queen of Sarees on Two Wheels

The Independence Day flag ride was an event I looked forward to every year, but this time felt different. It wasn't just about joining the ride; it was about making a personal statement, celebrating my identity, and honouring my roots. I decided to do something bold—ride in a saree that embodied the colours and spirit of the nation, symbolizing unity and freedom.

As I watched the days countdown to Independence Day, the idea of riding in a saree took hold of my mind. We at *Moto Riders*, decided to flaunt ethnic attires – atleast a kurti or a salwar kameez with tri colour dupatta. This wasn't just any ride—it was a tribute to freedom, both for the country and, in a way, for myself. I wanted my attire to reflect that sense of liberation, a harmonious blend of elegance, culture, and the thrill of the road. As a woman and a biker, this was my way of celebrating both my personal journey and the spirit of the nation.

The night before the ride, I stood in front of my wardrobe, rifling through sarees, my fingers brushing past the silks and cottons, each holding memories of different occasions. Then, my hand fell upon a tricolour saree, vibrant and full of life. The fabric was dotted with patches of handprints in the colours of the national flag—saffron, white, and green—scattered across the soft cloth. Each patch symbolized unity, freedom, and expression. It felt perfect, as if it had been waiting for this moment.

I paired it with a tribal print blouse, earthy in tones of beige and brown, simple yet grounding. Drape after drape, I experimented with ways to keep the saree functional, eventually styling it over my jeans, pulling it together with a sturdy corset belt that added a modern twist. The boots, gloves, and helmet completed the look, each piece chosen not only for safety but as part of a unique style statement that would stand out on the road.

The morning air was crisp and cool, holding that unique promise of an early August dawn. I carefully placed the national flag to the rear of my bike with the help of a curtain rod and some *jugaad*, ensuring it would catch the wind as I rode, fluttering with every turn and curve. I could feel the slight chill as I took a deep breath, savouring the quiet of the city before it fully woke up.

Helmet on, gloves fastened, I pressed the ignition, and the bike purred to life. The engine's gentle rumble felt like a heartbeat, syncing with my own excitement. For a moment, I just sat there, letting the RPM settle as I took in the feeling of the saree's fabric against me, blending femininity with the raw power of the bike.

As I pulled out of the driveway, the first rays of the sun were peeking over the horizon, casting a golden glow on the streets, still deserted except for a few early risers. The quietness of the morning felt sacred, a silent companion to my ride, and I felt a rare sense of peace settle within me as I made my way to the meetup point.

The streets gradually came alive as I rode through Hyderabad, the city beginning to stir with its usual energy. The sight of a woman on a bike always drew some attention, but the added element of a saree turned heads in a way that felt both exhilarating and heartwarming.

At a red light, I noticed a school bus pulling up beside me, filled with children in uniforms, their eyes widening in surprise and delight as they spotted me. A few of them started waving, their little hands pressing against the glass windows, mouths forming enthusiastic "hellos" and "hi didi!" Seeing their excitement, I waved back, smiling as their faces lit up with joy. It was a small moment, but it made my heart swell with happiness.

"Look, she's wearing a saree on a bike!" I overheard one of the teachers say to her colleague, both smiling as they watched me from the front of the bus. Their admiration was genuine, and it filled me with pride to be able to share this moment with them, embodying a celebration of tradition and strength.

As the light turned green, I continued onward, the saree fluttering in the wind, a unique rhythm that matched the hum of the bike. I could feel the fabric against my jeans, grounding me as I moved forward, each stretch of road bringing me closer to the meetup point and the day's celebration.

The meetup point was abuzz with energy as riders from different groups and backgrounds gathered, each one excited to start the day's ride. As I rode into the parking area, I felt the collective gaze of the group shift toward me. Eyes widened, smiles appeared, and nods of approval followed as they took in my attire—a saree, draped over jeans, cinched with a corset belt, and paired with rugged biker boots.

"Now that's a statement!" exclaimed a fellow rider who had always admired bold choices.

A few came over, their faces lighting up with admiration and curiosity. "You've outdone yourself today," Shweta said with a grin, patting my back. "This saree look with the flag is the most inspiring thing I've seen for a flag ride."

The camaraderie and shared patriotism felt tangible, each nod and smile a reminder that this was more than just a ride. We were celebrating our roots, our identities, and the freedom to express them.

As the engines roared to life and the group began its journey, I fell into formation, my bike gliding smoothly alongside others, all of us moving as one. The roads were still relatively quiet, and we took advantage of the open space, spreading out in synchronized rows, each bike proudly displaying the Indian flag.

The morning sun climbed higher, casting a warm glow over us as we made our way to the resort. Along the way, I caught glimpses of curious onlookers—shopkeepers standing at their doorways, elderly men out for morning walks, young children pointing and waving. The saree, the flags, the unity of bikers—it was a spectacle that drew admiration and respect from everyone who saw us.

The wind caught my saree, lifting it slightly, and I felt an indescribable joy in that moment. Riding in traditional attire, feeling both feminine and powerful, was a liberating experience. Each turn, each acceleration, felt like a testament to the strength of identity and the beauty of self-expression.

As we arrived at the resort, the event organizers welcomed us warmly, guiding us to an area set up for breakfast and a small ceremony. The group gathered, chatting, laughing, and exchanging stories from the ride. I could feel the energy of the group, the shared pride, and the joy of celebrating the nation's freedom together.

We were given small tokens—stickers, caps, and keychains—as mementos of the day. I glanced down at the sticker of the national flag and felt a swell of pride, knowing I would cherish this reminder of a day that was both meaningful and memorable.

Later, I slipped into the restroom to change, swapping my blouse and saree for a comfortable T-shirt that would make the ride back easier. As I folded the saree, I felt a lingering sense of accomplishment. It wasn't just a piece of fabric—it was a symbol of strength, a reminder that I had dared to be different, to celebrate my heritage while doing what I loved.

When I walked back out, I could still feel the memory of the saree draping me, as though it had become a part of me. The Independence Day flag ride had given me more than I expected. It was a day of unity, celebration, and the profound joy of being free to be myself on the road.

As we rode back, I held onto that feeling, the memory of waving school children, the admiration in the eyes of my fellow riders, and the fluttering of the national flag at the back of my bike. Each mile brought a sense of fulfilment, a pride that ran deep, a reminder that this journey was about more than just the road—it was about celebrating the spirit of independence, identity, and unity, all wrapped in the vibrant colours of freedom.

Man or Woman – Sill a Rider

Transitioning from one chapter of life to another, especially from living as a man to embracing life as a woman, is a profound transformation, yet my passion for riding remained unwavering. The road continued to teach me lessons in resilience, adaptability, and self-reflection, though the dynamics of riding changed in subtle but meaningful ways. Through all of it, my love for biking stayed a constant—a source of strength and joy that connected me to myself, to others, and to the world around me.

In this chapter, I reflect on how the journey evolved post-transition, how the world reacted, how my riding dynamics shifted, and, ultimately, how each lesson learned from the road became a powerful metaphor for life and personal growth.

Before my transition, resilience on the road meant pushing through physical challenges like weather, road conditions, and breakdowns. After transitioning, resilience took on new layers. Now, it wasn't just about handling the rain or enduring long rides—it was about facing social dynamics, handling occasional stares, and navigating a world that was sometimes curious, sometimes kind, and sometimes questioning.

There was one ride where resilience truly came into play. I was heading to a biker meetup, nervous about how I'd be perceived. I worried that people might see me differently, perhaps doubting my abilities because of my identity. But as the miles ticked by, my focus shifted back to the ride itself, the hum of the engine grounding me. Resilience became less about proving myself to others and more about staying true to my passion and pushing forward with confidence. The ride reaffirmed that my love for biking wasn't just about external validation—it was a journey of inner strength.

Transitioning taught me patience in a way the road never had before. The slow but meaningful process of self-discovery, the patience required to adapt, heal, and embrace each stage—it all felt reflected in my riding. Every mile became a metaphor for growth, a step closer to my authentic self, much like the journey of transition itself.

Post-transition, patience also took on a practical aspect. Riding as a transwoman meant occasionally dealing with situations where people's curiosity got the better of them. Sometimes at gas stations or rest stops, people would approach with questions—innocent curiosity, occasionally nosy stares. Learning to stay patient, answer kindly, or simply let them wonder became a small but meaningful part of the journey. Riding taught me to embrace these moments, seeing them as chances to show that my passion for the road was unchanged, and that who I am only adds depth to the ride.

Physically, riding as a woman brought changes that impacted my approach. Hormone therapy had reshaped my body subtly, affecting my weight distribution, strength, and centre of gravity. This meant adapting my riding style, handling the bike differently, adjusting my posture, and even reconsidering my choice of gear. It was an opportunity to reconnect with my bike, understanding its dynamics in new ways.

Riding became an exercise in adaptability, not only to the road but to my own evolving self. I learned to work with my body's changes, finding a new balance, adjusting my stance, and sometimes even my bike's settings, to fit my new physicality. The changes were practical, but they held a philosophical meaning too—accepting myself, adapting to change, and evolving in harmony with the world around me.

The biggest change post-transition was the kind of attention I received. In a community where riders often focus solely on the machine and the road, being a woman biker brought a different sort of curiosity. Some wondered if I'd face challenges riding, others had questions, and a few offered unsolicited advice.

One memorable experience happened during a group ride. A fellow rider, curious but cautious, asked, "Is it harder for you now?" His tone wasn't patronizing, just genuinely interested. I responded honestly, sharing that while there were some new dynamics to navigate, my love for riding was unchanged. By the end of the conversation, we shared a laugh, and I could see his perception shift from curiosity to admiration.

These interactions taught me to handle attention with grace, and over time, I noticed the initial surprise of others fading. They began seeing me as simply another passionate rider, and that acceptance was a testament to how the road brings people together, beyond identities and appearances.

Navigating routes remained an important skill, but post-transition, problem-solving extended beyond finding my way on the road. It now meant handling unexpected encounters, adapting to social dynamics, and finding my way in a world that had shifted just slightly around me.

There was a ride where my GPS lost signal as I traversed the rural roads between towns. Alone, and without the digital comfort of directions, I had to rely on instinct, memory, and the occasional help from friendly locals. I encountered a small village where people were fascinated by my attire, my bike, and, of course, the fact that I was riding solo.

Rather than feeling out of place, I approached them openly, asking for directions and even sharing smiles. The conversation became less about my identity and more about our shared humanity. Problem-solving wasn't just about navigation—it was about finding connections, breaking down assumptions, and embracing the unknown.

The solitude of riding offered a unique space for self-reflection, especially post-transition. Each mile became a chance to confront lingering insecurities, to work through fears, and to embrace the freedom that riding gave me. The road felt like a companion, a mirror that reflected my journey both on and off the bike.

One evening ride, as the sun set over a quiet stretch of highway, I found myself lost in thought. The gentle hum of the engine and the cool air brought a sense of calm, and I found myself confronting emotions I hadn't fully processed. Riding became a therapeutic experience, a safe space where I could face my thoughts and emotions without judgment. I realized that the road wasn't just a physical journey—it was a space for self-healing and acceptance.

Riding solo was a personal journey, but group rides brought their own lessons. Post-transition, joining group rides became a way of finding community, sharing experiences, and celebrating the joy of biking together. I discovered a new kind of camaraderie with fellow riders, and this sense of belonging was empowering.

On one such ride, a fellow biker Deekshitha joined me as we stopped for a rest. She turned to me, her face lit up with excitement, and said, "You inspire me. Seeing you on the road, being yourself—it makes me proud to be a woman and a rider." Her words reminded me that each ride wasn't just for myself; it was an opportunity to inspire others, to show that the road is for everyone. We continue to be good friends and sisters!

Group rides taught me the power of community—the comfort in shared experiences, the support from fellow riders, and the joy of celebrating each other's journeys. It was a reminder that, despite our individual paths, we are all bound by the same love for the open road.

Through all the changes, the essence of riding remained unchanged. The freedom, the thrill, the connection to the road—it was as powerful as ever. The road taught me that my passion for biking was beyond appearances or identities; it was a celebration of life itself.

On a ride through Gachibowli late one evening, as city lights blurred into streaks beside me, I felt an overwhelming sense of gratitude. The road had given me more than just the joy of riding—it had given me resilience, courage, and a deep sense of self-worth. Every turn, every mile, was a testament to the journey I had taken, both on the road and within myself.

Transitioning changed many things, but it didn't change my love for the road. If anything, it deepened it, adding new dimensions to my riding experience. The road taught me that life, much like a ride, is about embracing every turn, every change, and every unexpected stop. Each lesson learned on the road became a part of me, a reminder that no matter how much things change, the journey is as meaningful as ever.

Pushing Boundaries

Riding has always been my pathway to freedom, yet there are rides that push even the most seasoned bikers to their limits. These aren't just about hitting the open road; they involve navigating some of the most intense terrains, from high-altitude mountain passes to the slushy tracks of monsoon-soaked trails. Every bump, twist, and narrow escape serves as a reminder that true freedom lies in facing the unknown.

In this chapter, I recount two unforgettable experiences that pushed me beyond my comfort zone—my first true off-road encounter with the HYDE group at Ananthagiri Hills and a late-night ride that threw me into unfamiliar, conservative neighbourhoods. These rides didn't just test my endurance and mental toughness; they forced me to confront fear head-on and taught me powerful lessons in resilience, self-trust, and adaptability.

Every rider knows that certain journeys go beyond just getting from one point to another. These rides are adventures that challenge us, force us to learn new skills, and face fears we didn't know existed. Riding, for me, became a canvas to explore limits and navigate situations I would have never encountered otherwise. As my confidence grew, so did my willingness to face more extreme environments, and every encounter with a difficult ride brought me closer to understanding my resilience.

High-altitude, dense forests, deserts, or sudden rain—all environments hold their own challenges. While every ride has its unique demands, nothing could have prepared me for the times when even the environment seemed determined to test my mettle.

The HYDE group, known for its camaraderie and adventurous spirit, planned a group ride to Ananthagiri Hills, a beautiful location famed for its dense forests and serene landscapes. Eager to join, I set out with the group, thrilled at the thought of sharing this journey with fellow riders. The initial journey was smooth—a stretch of beautiful highways, gentle hills, and the familiar hum of engines accompanying us as we made our way into the hills.

Arriving at Ananthagiri, we were greeted by the cool morning air, the hills veiled in mist, and a landscape so pristine that it felt untouched. I thought our ride had reached its pinnacle, but little did I know, we were just getting started. The group decided to extend the journey to a nearby reservoir, which sounded perfect—until they mentioned a few patches of off-road terrain.

I was, and still am, a rider who feels at home on highways. My bike is built for speed and smooth roads, and off-roading isn't just unfamiliar—it's challenging on my machine.

But the group's encouragement spurred me forward, and I decided to go along, not yet aware of the obstacles awaiting us. The journey toward the reservoir began smoothly, the roads gradually narrowing and becoming rougher. Then, the first obstacle appeared a stretch of thick, slushy mud that seemed determined to swallow any tire that dared to cross it. I stopped as I saw the other riders cross, their wheels fishtailing and mud splattering with each spin. My heart raced as I considered the risks. My bike wasn't designed for off-road slush, and I questioned my ability to make it through.
As I hesitated, one of the riders, KM, noticed and waited, offering a reassuring smile. "You've got this," he said, dismounting to help guide me through the patch. His calm confidence and patient encouragement reminded me that I wasn't alone. "The track ahead is clearer, don't worry about this small stretch," he said, and that reassurance was all I needed.

Summoning courage, I whispered a quick prayer to Hanuman Ji and started inching forward, gripping the handlebars and steadying my breathing. My tires slid in the mud, the bike swaying with each push, but I kept my focus, trusting that I had the control to pull through. My nerves melted into exhilaration as I made it to the other side, triumphant. This wasn't just a small victory; it was a personal achievement, showing me that fear could be overcome with patience, determination, and support from others.

With my newfound confidence, I felt ready for anything. The next two patches of rough terrain were easier to cross, each one reinforcing the sense of accomplishment. With every pass, I felt my confidence growing, the fear melting away, and a quiet pride settling in its place. These weren't just muddy paths—they were tests of resilience and focus, challenges that forced me to concentrate on each small action while trusting my instincts.

However, the final patch was a true beast, a stretch of deep, dark mud that swallowed nearly a quarter of the tires of the bikes that attempted it. Seeing the sheer depth, I knew that my bike wouldn't make it. I parked, walking the remaining 200 meters to the reservoir, my boots squelching in the mud as I approached the serene waters where the other bikes were parked. The scene was beautiful—a line of bikes against the reservoir, the mist swirling around us, reflecting a sense of peace after the rough terrain.

Standing there, gazing at the reflection of the bikes in the water, I felt a pull. I had come so far, crossed so many patches of mud—how could I let this last stretch stop me?

I returned to my bike, steeling myself to face the final obstacle. As I navigated it, feeling the bike struggle through the deep mud, my confidence surged. I made it to the reservoir, my bike parked proudly alongside the others. That day, I learned that boundaries are meant to be pushed, and that resilience often lies just beyond the limits of fear.

Fear is an inseparable part of riding. It creeps up in moments when control feels tenuous—especially when the environment changes unexpectedly. Another unforgettable experience happened one evening when I was heading to a candle march organised by *Telangana Women Moto Bikers*. I was dressed in a simple black salwar kameez, setting out on a route recommended by Google Maps. Little did I know it would lead me through unfamiliar gullies and conservative neighbourhoods.

As I made my way through narrow, poorly lit lanes, unease started to build. I could feel the stares of curious onlookers, and soon, a few people on bikes seemed to be slowing down, matching my pace. An autorickshaw trailed behind, and I sensed that I had attracted some attention I wasn't comfortable with. I glanced around, realizing that turning back wasn't an option anymore—I was committed to the path.

My heart pounded as I maintained my composure, gripping the handlebars and focusing on the road ahead. It felt like time had slowed, every glance and shadow stretching the journey longer than it was. In my mind, I kept reassuring myself to stay calm and collected, that reaching the main road was the only option. Finally, the lights of the main road emerged, and relief washed over me as I pulled into a well-lit area.

I parked at a nearby footpath, taking a moment to gather myself, my pulse gradually calming. That ride taught me to navigate not just physical obstacles but emotional ones, teaching me that courage is sometimes about pushing through fear with steady resolve.

Each of these experiences brought its own lessons. The slushy off-road patch at Ananthagiri taught me resilience—the determination to keep going even when the terrain felt impossible. The ride through unfamiliar streets reminded me of the importance of self-trust, of maintaining composure in the face of fear.

Riding teaches resilience, both on the road and in life. It teaches us to trust our instincts, to believe in our abilities even when the world seems challenging. Navigating challenging roads has given me the skill to assess risks, the patience to adapt to unexpected changes, and the courage to face my fears without backing down.

Pushing physical and mental limits on the road brought me face-to-face with my inner strength. Overcoming these challenges became personal milestones, markers of growth and self-discovery. The sense of pride and fulfilment from parking my bike by the reservoir was profound—it wasn't just about reaching the destination; it was about proving to myself that I could achieve more than I thought possible.

As a woman rider, breaking boundaries meant more than just conquering terrain; it was about navigating societal expectations, understanding my own limits, and ultimately celebrating the joy and freedom of the ride. Each boundary crossed was a testament to the strength within, a reminder that fear can be the gateway to resilience.

The road, with all its unpredictability, taught me that boundaries are merely stepping stones toward self-discovery. Extreme environments pushed me to grow, to learn, and to embrace the strength that lies beyond fear. Riding isn't just a journey from one place to another—it's a journey within, a path that reveals the resilience, courage, and freedom we hold within ourselves.

Every ride, every challenging patch, has shown me that the world outside mirrors the world within, and by pushing boundaries, we uncover our truest selves.

Support & Inspiration

Starting out in the biker community, embracing both my femininity and a strong sense of fashion meant stepping into the unknown. Biking groups often have unwritten rules about what a "real biker" should look like, and at first, I could feel the skepticism from fellow riders. Some questioned my practical choices, others seemed simply intrigued by the sight of a biker in a skater dress or well-tailored jeans. Many wondered if my outfits were safe, if my approach was serious, and if I was there to make a statement or for the love of riding itself.

These reactions, while mixed, didn't deter me. The combination of fashion and riding had always felt natural to me, and every time I rode in my chosen attire, it was a step toward merging two important parts of my life. The thrill of the ride met with my passion for style, blending seamlessly into a kind of personal self-expression that felt right. I saw riding as more than a hobby; it was an extension of my identity and expressing it through my appearance was a part of that joy.

Over time, I noticed that many of these initial doubts began to fade. Fellow riders saw that my commitment to riding was no passing phase, nor was my passion for personal style something superficial. I took my safety as seriously as my appearance, investing in high-quality gear, boots, and jackets that offered protection while allowing me to stay true to myself.

One of the pivotal moments for me was on a group ride, where I arrived in fitted jeans, a comfortable but stylish crop top under my riding jacket, and my favourite pair of long boots. After the ride, an experienced rider approached me, looking genuinely impressed. “I didn’t think anyone could pull that off and still handle the road like you did,” he admitted, clearly surprised and impressed. The subtle respect in his words meant a lot; it was a reminder that skill and individuality could go together on the open road.

This gradual shift in acceptance opened doors for others, too. The biker groups I rode with, like *TWMB*, was founded and led by strong women with a passion for bikes and a desire to foster inclusivity within the biker community. Seeing their confidence in their unique styles inspired me, and I, in turn, hoped to inspire others. They showed that there was room for everyone, regardless of how they chose to present themselves.

The best part of this journey was watching others embrace their own individuality. Some riders began adding personal touches to their gear—a pop of colour on their jackets, more form-fitting outfits, or experimenting with accessories that reflected their own style. The biker stereotype was starting to change within my circles, proving that riding was about freedom, both in movement and self-expression.

One of the most heartwarming outcomes of staying true to myself on the road has been the impact on other women, especially younger riders. It became clear over time that my presence as a biker who embraced her femininity and style wasn't just about my own freedom; it had a ripple effect, encouraging others to pursue their passion for riding without feeling pressured to fit a particular mold.

After a group ride one day, a young woman approached me, her eyes sparkling with admiration. "I always thought riding meant giving up my sense of style, like I had to look tough to be taken seriously," she said. "Seeing you out there, riding with such confidence and still embracing who you are, has made me realize I can do it too." Her words hit close to home, and I could feel the sincerity in her voice. She didn't just see a fellow biker; she saw someone living proof that she could follow her own path.

Moments like these underscored the fact that riding was about more than the open road; it was about showing women that they didn't have to conform. Each time a woman or a young girl approached me with stories of wanting to ride, I felt grateful to be a small part of their journey.

A particularly touching moment happened when a father introduced me to his teenage daughter at an event. "She looks up to you," he said, smiling proudly. "She wants to ride, and she tells me you've shown her it's possible." His daughter, brimming with excitement, looked up at me, her gaze filled with admiration. She didn't just want to ride; she wanted to ride with the same confidence and individuality I brought to the road. Seeing that spark in her eyes was a reminder that our influence often goes beyond the miles we ride.

Women's biker groups like *Telangana Women Moto Bikers*, *Bikerni Hyderabad* and *Valkyrie*, founded by inspirational women like Shweta, Anisah and Sheba, have been instrumental in breaking down stereotypes and creating supportive spaces for female riders. These groups encouraged women to embrace biking not as something they had to adjust for but as something they could adapt to suit themselves. Through training sessions, mentorship, and community rides, these groups opened doors for women to ride in a way that felt natural to them.

I met incredible women in these groups, each with her unique style and approach to riding. There was Shweta, a woman who could organize rides with seamless precision and somehow make everyone feel included and supported. Sheba, a strong woman, with far sightedness and a passion for riding. These women, and so many others, taught me that riding wasn't about conformity; it was about the freedom to express, connect, and celebrate each other's strengths.

Through these groups, I met women who had always wanted to ride but never felt they could until they found a community. We shared stories, tips on gear, and even recommendations on stylish yet practical outfits. Each woman brought her own story, and together, we created a culture where individuality was celebrated. The growth and confidence I saw in others inspired me to keep pushing forward, knowing that each ride was part of something bigger than myself.

One of the most significant aspects of my journey has been redefining the image of a "biker" by embracing fashion, femininity, and strength in a way that feels authentic. The conventional biker look is powerful, but I was eager to show that a feminine and stylish look could be just as fierce, powerful, and road ready.

During one meet-up, a teenage girl came up to me, fascinated by my outfit—a well-fitted jacket over a comfortable crop top paired with high-waist jeans and protective gear. She commented on how “cool” it looked and how she’d never thought someone could ride a bike looking so feminine yet powerful. That admiration was a reminder that we’re breaking barriers, each outfit and every ride reshaping perceptions.

Riding has always been a celebration of freedom, and I realized that I was helping to create a new narrative for what a “real biker” could look like. There was something empowering about proving that a biker didn’t need to look or act a certain way; they just needed the courage to embrace who they were.

Over time, the influence spread beyond the immediate biker circles. I started receiving messages from women who were hesitant riders, those who had wanted to ride for years but felt pressured by family or societal expectations. They saw my posts, read about my rides, and began to wonder if they could step into the world of biking on their own terms.

One woman wrote to me saying, "Seeing you embrace riding your way gave me the courage to believe I can do the same." These messages reminded me of my own journey, the challenges, and the hesitation I felt at the beginning. Each response became a small act of encouragement, my way of giving back to a community that had shaped me.

At biking events, I started meeting these women face-to-face, each with her unique background and reason for wanting to ride. Whether they were college students, mothers, or professionals, our conversations were filled with stories of dreams, fears, and determination. Together, we formed bonds that went beyond riding; it was a shared journey of self-discovery and empowerment.

Over time, the reactions from the community became a powerful source of inspiration. The initial scepticism turned into support, curiosity transformed into admiration, and the impact extended beyond my own experiences on the road. Embracing my unique style on the bike became a reminder to others—and myself—that the road is a place of freedom, strength, and individuality.

As I look back on the faces, the stories, and the words of encouragement, I feel a renewed sense of purpose. The journey of breaking stereotypes, inspiring women, and forming connections has shown me that riding is more than a hobby—it's a means of self-expression, a movement, and a celebration of the uniqueness each rider brings to the road.

Vision, Evolution, Legacy

Riding a bike is, at its heart, so much more than getting from point A to point B. For those of us who have been touched by the freedom of the road, it's a journey within—a way to find ourselves, embrace new challenges, and escape the complexities of daily life. In my vision for the future of the biker community, I see riders becoming not just individuals on a path but a collective force for unity, passion, and positive change.

As I reflect on my own journey and look forward to the next generation of riders, I am filled with hope and purpose. The biker community isn't just a niche; it's a movement, and every rider is an ambassador, carrying the message of freedom, respect, and safe exploration wherever they go.

Riding didn't start as the passion-driven culture it has evolved into today. For many, bikes were simply tools—affordable, practical machines for getting to work, school, or running errands. But somewhere along the line, this utilitarian approach evolved. People began to understand that the journey could be just as rewarding as the destination. In the early days, motorcycles were transformed into symbols of speed and thrill through racing, with events like the Isle of Man TT capturing imaginations. The cafe racer culture of the 1960s in Britain, for example, marked a unique point where bikes became not just vehicles but statements of individuality and rebellion, a form of identity that resonated with the youth.

Riding became about quick escapes, late-night rides, and the thrill of going full throttle down empty streets. Today, bikes have evolved beyond their mechanical frames. For many, riding has become a form of meditation, a way to disconnect from the noise of the world and be alone with oneself. Modern riders aren't simply chasing speed; they're chasing something deeper—adventure, connection, and meaning. And this is the spirit I hope will continue to grow, transforming riding into a journey of self-discovery, exploration, and joy for the generations to come.

Riding has an almost mystical quality—it simplifies life. When you're on the road, there's a single focus, a clarity that cuts through the usual clutter of thoughts, worries, and responsibilities. It's just you, the bike, and the open road ahead. For so many, me included, riding is a form of escape, a moment of peace in an otherwise chaotic world.

I dream of a future where biking communities grow as sanctuaries for those seeking solace from life's turbulence. I envision more safe, organized spaces where riders can gather, share stories, laugh over shared experiences, and find that pure joy that riding brings. A thriving community can offer something powerful to its members—an escape, a sense of belonging, and a support system that's there both on and off the road.

As more people recognize the emotional and mental benefits of riding, I hope society will begin to understand the transformative power of the bike. I see riding as a therapeutic release, a way to shed the weight of everyday life, even if just for a while. The biker community has the potential to be a space where people find strength and peace, where the pressures of the world fade, leaving only the hum of the engine and the open road.

I see a future where the biker community isn't just about rides and rallies but about contributing to the world. There's a strength in numbers, and with so many passionate riders united by a love for the road, we can become a significant force for good. Imagine a world where biker communities across cities and countries are known for their charity rides, environmental initiatives, or campaigns to promote road safety.

Groups like "*TWMB*", "*Bikerni Hyderabad*" and *Valkyrie*, founded by female riders, are already creating a lasting impact by encouraging more women to ride and inspiring a culture of inclusion. Their impact isn't just in the number of members but in the barriers they break down, proving that biking is for anyone who has the heart for it. Through education and outreach, these communities can change perceptions, showing that biking isn't just a reckless pursuit of adrenaline but a powerful, constructive force.

In this vision, I see biker groups becoming known for community service, using our collective power to fundraise for causes, promote local businesses, and give back to the neighborhoods that serve as the backdrop for our rides. Groups like *Cerberus, ATH, HUB, Freedom Riding Club, HYDE, Kirak Riders* etc have done more than what could be expected out of them in nurturing the culture of biking. Whether it's a flag ride to promote unity, a gathering to raise awareness for road safety, or simply beautifying our community by organizing clean-up rides, I hope to see bikers leading with purpose.

One of the things I hold most dearly in my vision for the biker community is a stronger emphasis on safety. While the thrill of riding is undeniable, safety is the foundation upon which we build our love for the road. I dream of a future where every rider, regardless of their background or experience, values and respects the importance of protective gear, disciplined riding, and adhering to traffic laws.

Riding without proper safety equipment or recklessly weaving through traffic puts not just the rider but others on the road in danger. I believe that the future of the biker community lies in responsible riding, in riders looking out for one another and cultivating a mindset that respects the road and the lives on it.

Biker communities, with their platforms and influence, can play an instrumental role in promoting safe riding. By organizing workshops on safe riding practices, encouraging helmet use, and creating a culture where responsible riding is celebrated, we can set an example for new riders. I envision a community that leads by example, where safety is seen not as a hindrance but as an essential part of the thrill and freedom that comes with riding.

Despite its evolution, biking is often met with a mix of awe and judgment. Some still view bikers as reckless or rebellious, stereotypes that don't reflect the passion, skill, and dedication that so many riders bring to the road. In my vision, I see a future where society's view of bikers shifts, where we are recognized not as outliers but as respected individuals who contribute to the community.
I want the next generation of riders to enjoy respect from society, not only for their love of riding but for the values they uphold. I imagine a world where being a biker is as respected as any other pursuit, where people see bikers as diverse individuals who share a love for the open road. As we continue to ride responsibly, support charitable causes, and contribute to society, I hope society will come to see the biker community as a positive, uplifting force.

Biker clubs can lead this shift by encouraging community engagement, holding open events that welcome non-riders, and building bonds with local residents and authorities. This bridge-building is essential to changing public perceptions and allowing the world to see bikers as a supportive, welcoming, and valuable part of society.

The biker community, though more inclusive than ever, still has strides to make in becoming a truly welcoming space for everyone. I envision a future where female riders, younger bikers, and people from all walks of life feel safe, respected, and empowered to join and thrive in the community. Groups like *Bikerni Hyderabad* and *TWMB* have been trailblazers in creating space for women in the biking world. Bikerni Hyderabad has been active since 2013 and many of their ladies have crossed international borders as well! Jai Bharathi, Seema, and Anisah Latheef, of the *Bikerni Hyderabad* have inspired so many women along their journey and are definitely the pioneers in motivating women riders. I still remember coming across Anisah's post on Instagram where she stood proudly with her bike in Ladakh. That picture was immensely powerful and motivated me to get going with my riding life! Similarly, Shweta with her go getter attitude has brought hundreds of women together who share a common passion for riding! I hope to see more such groups grow.

It's crucial for the next generation of riders to inherit a community that is respectful and inclusive. For women who might face hesitations or even obstacles in embracing riding, biker communities can provide the support, training, and camaraderie needed to help them start their journey. And for young riders, I hope we can foster a space that values mentorship, guiding them on safe and responsible riding practices.

In this vision, biker communities serve as families, as safe spaces where riders can be vulnerable, seek guidance, and find support. As riders, we can be role models for the next generation, teaching them to not only love the ride but respect it.

As I look ahead, my heart fills with hope for what the future holds. Biking has been a source of joy, strength, and identity, and my vision is for the biker community to become a force of unity, passion, and change. I hope for a world where riders are seen as individuals who respect the road, cherish freedom, and seek adventure not just for themselves but to inspire others.

Each ride is a chance to explore, to connect, to push boundaries, and to leave a legacy. The biker community of the future is one where riders support one another, contribute to society, and uphold values that reflect the beauty of the road. I dream of a world where bikers aren't just seen as thrill-seekers but as thoughtful, passionate individuals who embody resilience, freedom, and purpose.

This vision is more than a hope—it's a call to action. To every rider reading this, I urge you to be part of this future, to make riding a symbol of unity, respect, and responsible exploration. As we ride forward, may we remember that every journey, every turn, and every road we travel is an opportunity to make the biker community stronger, more inclusive, and more meaningful than ever before.

www.ingramcontent.com/pod-product-compliance
Lightning Source LLC
LaVergne TN
LVHW021147160826
845679LV00024B/2076

* 9 7 9 8 8 9 6 3 2 2 1 7 7 *